Praise for *Reducing School Expenses*

"I have known Dr. Clinton Born for many years and have taken numerous classes under him. His information has always proven to be highly accurate, up to date, and on the pulse of what is currently happening in education. Dr. Born's book, *Reducing School Expenses: Containing Insurance Costs, Funding Capital, and Tackling the Challenges*, does an outstanding job of explaining the details of district-level finances. I believe this text will prove invaluable to central office administrators just starting their careers and will be a useful resource for the experienced administrator. The state-by-state comparisons in tables are eye opening and are information I plan to use in conversations with my legislator while lobbying for improvements to our state's funding model. The superintendent, chief financial officer, and school board members have a legal and moral obligation to be good stewards of the monies entrusted to them; this text is a 'must-have' edition for every administrator's bookshelf."

—**John L. Belt**, assistant superintendent,
Indian Creek Local School District, Wintersville, Ohio

"This book confronts the risks and addresses the potential challenges that superintendents, CFOs, and human resources directors face as stewards of school district's financial resources. If you need practical advice on how to handle your school district's finances, look no further. Like every social, political, and economic policy in our country, health insurance is complicated. Chapter 2 is a master class in employee benefits and risk management. Further, Dr. Born's clear and concise definitions of terms throughout the book simplify complex concepts for the reader leading to a greater understanding that will help them make better decisions. *Reducing School Expenses: Containing Insurance Costs, Funding Capital, and Tackling the Challenges* is not only a timely book, it's essential reading for every superintendent, CFO, and human resources director in the field of education. This thoughtfully organized and theoretically sound book will empower educational leaders with the tools they need to navigate the world of school finance."

—**Leslie Scott**, Human Resources director for SKC, Inc., former HR director for Pressley Ridge and Propel Schools, Pittsburgh, Pennsylvania

"Dr. Born's book, *Reducing School Expenses: Containing Insurance Costs, Funding Capital, and Tackling the Challenges*, provides a comprehensive look into school finance issues from a national lens and is conducive to practical application. Current and aspiring administrators, both building and district level, will find the content useful for future planning and more routine practices or daily reference. His chapter 2 work on employee benefits and risk management is critically important, but a topic that is often overlooked. The projects in each chapter offer the reader an opportunity to extend topic understanding and application. The reference section is especially thorough, permitting the inspired reader a springboard for additional investigation."

—**Mark Furda**, director of Graduate Education, Franciscan University of Steubenville, Steubenville, Ohio

"The intensive and in-depth research in this book is a unique and fantastic analysis of school finance. The realistic and practical approach is refreshing and is a true-to-life snapshot of how all facets of school finance affect daily operations. In particular, I found the 'outside the box' thinking surrounding health insurance compelling. It is clear that Dr. Born's experience and research have created a 'must-have' resource for any school leader."

—**Richard A. Hall**, PhD, superintendent, Mid-East Career and Technology Centers, Zanesville, Ohio

"Dr. Born's *Reducing School Expenses: Containing Insurance Costs, Funding Capital, and Tackling the Challenges* is a comprehensive look at the major financial issues facing school administrators. His years of experience and study provide guidance on a wide variety of areas. Most notable are the links to individual state policies, which make this guide applicable to school leaders across the nation. As an administrator of a nonpublic school, I especially appreciated his coverage of issues that affect nonpublic and public charters, which makes this text unique."

—**Theresa Danaher**, principal, Bishop Mussio Schools, Steubenville, Ohio

Reducing School Expenses

Reducing School Expenses

Containing Insurance Costs, Funding Capital, and Tackling the Challenges

Clinton Born

Published in partnership with the
Association of School Business Officials International (ASBO)

Published in partnership with the
Association of School Business Officials International (ASBO)

Published by Rowman & Littlefield
An imprint of The Rowman & Littlefield Publishing Group, Inc.
4501 Forbes Boulevard, Suite 200, Lanham, Maryland 20706
www.rowman.com

6 Tinworth Street, London SE11 5AL, United Kingdom

British Library Cataloguing in Publication Information Available

Library of Congress Cataloging-in-Publication Data
Names: Born, Clinton, 1948- author.
Title: Reducing school expenses : containing insurance costs, funding capital, and tackling the challenges / Clinton Born.
Description: Lanham : Rowman & Littlefield, [2020] | Includes bibliographical references and index. | Summary: "Reducing School Expenses recommends research-supported solutions on specific topics to reduce school expenses; contain health insurance, pension, and risk management costs; fund capital projects; and tackle critical funding issues in primary and secondary public, nonpublic, and charter schools"—Provided by publisher.
Identifiers: LCCN 2020010338 (print) | LCCN 2020010339 (ebook) | ISBN 9781475856682 (cloth) | ISBN 9781475856699 (paperback) | ISBN 9781475856705 (ebook)
Subjects: LCSH: Education—Finance. | Education—Costs. | Educational planning.
Classification: LCC LB2824 .B656 2020 (print) | LCC LB2824 (ebook) | DDC 371.2/06—dc23
LC record available at https://lccn.loc.gov/2020010338
LC ebook record available at https://lccn.loc.gov/2020010339

∞™ The paper used in this publication meets the minimum requirements of American National Standard for Information Sciences – Permanence of Paper for Printed Library Materials, ANSI/NISO Z39.48-1992.

To my dear, departed parents who inspired my life accomplishments—Doris I. and Clayton W. Born, Sr.—and my loving wife, Monna Born, who supports my endeavors and endures my endless hours on the Internet and computer.

Contents

Foreword

For current and future school administrators across the country who desire a positive impact on their districts and communities, *Reducing School Expenses: Containing Insurance Costs, Funding Capital, and Tackling the Challenges* is a worthwhile read. This book presents pragmatic strategies and offers evidence-based solutions on specific topics, particularly resource management and capital investments, that no other school finance text advances.

Dr. Born, the author, was one of my professors while obtaining licensure for administration, and his knowledge and experiences have helped many of his students rise quickly to chief executive roles in schools served by Franciscan University of Steubenville, especially in the tristate geographical area of Ohio, Pennsylvania, and West Virginia.

As a school administrator, I started my career as a middle school principal in a rural community. After that year, I was an assistant superintendent in two school districts for a six-year stint. Following those appointments, I served as a superintendent of schools. Subsequently, I was designated as a county superintendent for an Educational Service Agency before settling into my current role as a chief executive officer for a multistate self-insurance consortium. Within the context of my professional career, I also cofounded a charter school and worked in private, vocational, and prison systems. In each of the aforementioned positions, I applied the principles espoused by Dr. Born and addressed in this book.

Chapter 1, for instance, considers best practices in purchasing school resources and obtaining price quotations, requests for proposal, and competitive sealed bids, which are vital functions for today's school administrators. Each school deserves the best prices for products and services through superlative budget execution, and this chapter delivers the content for such accomplishments.

Chapter 2, a practical guide for insurance terms, definitions, and cost-saving strategies, explains fringe benefits that state or federal laws statutorily mandate districts provide and others that districts voluntarily offer employees. This chapter also describes risk insurances (i.e., commercial property, general liability, and fleet) that district officials must administer to carry out school activities. Because these insurances are a significant part of a district's budget and costs continue to skyrocket, these initiatives should be well understood by school executives, which this book successfully explains.

Based on my experiences, other school finance texts and administration training programs do not provide practical applications for insurance management, including specific cost-containment strategies. For instance, a self-insured school district saves 15% to 20% on premiums that typically profit the insurance company. This book details substance to educate aspiring and practicing school leaders on cost-efficient human resource implementation and risk management with substantiated results to control costs.

School administrators will inevitably face building projects for improvement, repair, or new construction. Chapter 3 reports the activities and applications that public, nonpublic, and public charter districts must pursue to secure local, state, and federal funding; renovate an existing structure; and build a new building. This chapter clarifies each process on a state-by-state basis in straightforward detail. Successfully securing bond funding for a district is an example clearly described in this chapter.

Chapter 4 examines the means to establish a fair, sound tax system and underscores the effects that primary and secondary education budget cuts exhibit on student academic performances. This section also explores the escalating costs of employee health care, pensions, special education services, and textbooks; confirms the negative force of unfunded and underfunded mandates on student achievement; and analyzes the methods to sustain adequate and equitable fund distribution.

This chapter offers policymakers and school officials research-supported suggestions to tackle each critical funding issue and maximize efficiencies despite difficulties. Because funding from local, state, and federal resources remains limited, a school administrator *must* effectively manage the largest portion of a district budget—salary and benefits.

Reducing School Expenses: Containing Insurance Costs, Funding Capital, and Tackling the Challenges with state-by-state comparisons offers powerful data to investigate primary and secondary school funding. Each chapter addresses issues related to nonpublic and public charter schools, including the challenges that officials face regarding funding for these schools. Without doubt, this extensively researched book is priceless for aspiring and practicing school officials.

Dr. George Ash

Chief Executive Officer

Jefferson Health Plan

Steubenville, Ohio

Preface

School leaders today, whether in a public, nonpublic, or charter school, should administer their schools as keen business executives due to a multitude of fiscal demands on school operations. Based upon the author's years of school administrative experience, real-world application, and extensive research, this book, *Reducing School Expenses: Containing Insurance Costs, Funding Capital, and Tackling the Challenges*, describes superlative practices to reduce district expenses, investigates soaring fringe benefit and risk management insurance costs, clarifies capital funding sources, and explores persistent school finance challenges.

In today's economic climate, aspiring and practicing school administrators, chief fiscal officers, and board members, tasked with financial responsibilities, should "get the most bang for the buck" by utilizing best business practices because money is always tight. School officials must cost-effectively offer employee fringe benefits and district risk hazard insurances to protect district assets because these costs represent almost 25% of a district's budget with continual rising expenses on the horizon. School officials should be aware of the means to secure local, state, and federal capital funding when necessary.

Readers must be alerted to the school finance challenges that face public, nonpublic, and charter school officials and should be aware of the evidence-based solutions to tackle each of the following critical issues:

- equitable local, state, and federal taxation systems to fund public services, including education;
- escalating costs related to employee health insurance, pension assurance, special education services, and textbooks;
- state and federal budget cuts;

- effects of unfunded and underfunded mandates; and
- adequate and equitable fund distribution systems.

After scanning the market of school finance textbooks, a definite need surfaced to deliver a text that distinctly addresses these topics, particularly evidence-based employee health insurance cost-containment measures and recommendations for school officials as well as policymakers to tackle each challenge. In addition, because a void exists in texts for officials at nonpublic and public charter schools on these matters, a content requisite was evident as well. Objectives open each chapter aligned to the National Policy Board for Educational Administration standards (2018)—*National Educational Leadership Preparation* (NELP) *Recognition Standards: District Level*—which may be retrieved from www.npbea.org.

This resource will benefit readers through

- public, nonpublic, and charter schools specific content for each reader's situation;
- authentic, end-of-chapter projects to extend and apply readers' understandings; and
- numerous tables to differentiate substance because each topic warrants unique consideration based on the readers' physical location and particular circumstance.

Enjoy the text and advance your comprehension by reducing district expenses, containing insurance costs, funding capital investments, and tackling the school finance challenges!

Acknowledgments

I express my appreciation to several individuals who contributed to the development of this book. I am extremely thankful for Sandra Nelms, editor, who suggested significant writing improvements to the text and dramatically advanced my writing skill. I also value Dr. George Ash, who read and offered suggestions for chapter 2 content regarding employee benefits and risk management insurances.

Chapter 1

Procurement

OBJECTIVES

After reading this chapter, you should be able to

- ✓ explain proper district purchase order procedures (NELP 3.3, 6.1, 7.2, 7.3);
- ✓ describe the advantages and disadvantages of specific procurement practices and apply cost-efficient purchasing applications (NELP 3.3, 6.1, 6.2, 7.2, 7.3, 7.4); and
- ✓ understand and properly execute the procedures for obtaining a price quotation and a competitive as well as sealed bid (NELP 3.3, 6.1, 6.2, 7.2, 7.3, 7.4).

Elementary and secondary school systems in the United States spent $694.2 billion on education during the 2017 fiscal year, which is the most current Census Bureau data at the time of this publication (U.S. Census Bureau, 2019a). This volume of expenditures illustrates that public, nonpublic, and public charter schools possess massive buying power. School procurement demands systematic, well-established processes to discover, acquire, and evaluate resources (i.e., materials, supplies, equipment, and services) for students' learning needs and staff work (McFarland et al., 2019).

Precise procurement also supports financial accountability by accurately recording transactions and efficiently locating the best resources at the lowest, reasonable prices. Associated district policies and regulations, in line with federal and state laws, detail uniform procurement procedures for administrators, staff, vendors, and patrons to perform properly on a daily basis. These policies clarify functions, legalize actions, and relieve pressure on employees to make sound buying decisions under the constraint of time and expediency (Brimley, Verstegen, & Knoeppel, 2020).

Individuals often articulate procurement and purchasing as interchangeable terms, although these expressions hold different meanings. Procurement encompasses several overarching business activities that involve the acquisition of resources—letting contracts, establishing contract terms and conditions, selecting vendors, as well as vetting and obtaining resources. Purchasing, by contrast, includes a subset of procurement that simply expresses buying, receiving, and paying for resources (Bhuvaneswaran, 2018).

To implement district procurement goals that complement the educational mission, school personnel should

- recognize, administer, and adhere strictly to board policies, state statutes, and federal laws;
- perform with the highest professional and ethical standards;
- procure quality resources with the best value through efficient and expeditious methods;
- execute electronic procedures that comply with federal, state, and local regulations; and
- process all purchases and competitive bids in an honest, fair, and transparent manner without conflicts of interest, improprieties, or personal gains (Association of School Business Officials International, 2019).

Although school administrators maintain limited control over the revenue that a district obtains, they more easily influence district spending decisions. Because modern times dictate "doing more with less" money and staff, each dollar counts. School administrators, therefore, should investigate tactics to uncover financial savings, optimize resource utilization, and be resourceful.

Consequently, sound business practices that emphasize legal, expert procurement processes and procedures stand as critical intelligences for school leaders. To execute policies in effectively managing expenses, Dunn (2018) recommended that school administrators must

- understand and stay abreast of related federal and state laws;
- review and annually amend accompanying in-house policies, procedures, and processes;
- appraise and accordingly modify supporting forms and contracts;
- develop, adopt, and maintain an accessible procurement/purchasing manual;

- educate the staff on district procurement and purchasing routines;
- ensure that staff members understand employee procurement roles and levels of authority;
- anticipate district and school building needs;
- compare, analyze, and systematically assess resources and expenditure costs; and
- purchase the best-valued resources at the right time and position the assets in the proper location.

EXPENDITURES

The U.S. primary and secondary schools spent $610.3 billion on operations during the 2017 fiscal year, which is the most current Census Bureau data at the time of publication. Nationally, salaries were the largest expenditure for school districts with $343 billion spent on wages, which represented 56.2% of the total expenses. Employee benefits, the second largest cost, denoted 23.7% of the spending sum or $144.5 billion (U.S. Census Bureau, 2019a).

The combined expenditures for salary plus benefits typically average 80% to 85% of a district's entire spending; these percentages characterize a typical service-oriented industry. When a district spends above 85% of the total budget on salary and benefits, the district stands in financial crisis (Leader, 2019).

Purchased services (e.g., contracts for utilities, technology maintenance, legal counsel, and other external agreements) accounted for 11% of the total U.S. school spending in the 2017 fiscal year. Paper, workbooks, and cleaning products (i.e., supplies) comprised 8% of the complete school expenses in the United States. Capital outlay (e.g., expenditures for property acquisition, equipment, vehicles, building renovations, or new construction) was the remaining 2% of the complete expenditures for districts in the United States. Interest on debt for obligations (e.g., bonds) portrayed another capital outlay (McFarland et al., 2019).

Compulsory collective bargaining agreements in unionized districts across the country greatly impact a district's fiscal operation. The school board sets the direction for collective bargaining with input from the superintendent, treasurer/chief fiscal officer (CFO), primary negotiators, legal counsel, administrators, and fiscal advisors. Because school officials hold such an enormous fiduciary responsibility, they should assure the public that union bargaining with employees will not exceedingly divert too many dollars from student learning (Michigan Association of School Boards, 2018).

Using guidance from key sources (i.e., legal counsel, negotiators, superintendent, school business manager, and/or CFO/treasurer), school boards should maintain personnel contract agreements with clauses that explicitly proclaim management rights to accentuate integral school board and administrative duties (Michigan Association of School Boards, 2018).

With regard to economic subjects in negotiated agreements, the board should set parameters on the contract's financial components prior to negotiations, including the available dollars for contract settlement. These restrictions should be closely coordinated with the business office in order to certify accuracy (Michigan Association of School Boards, 2018).

Calculating contract proposals, analyzing various salary packages, and developing insurance cost-containment strategies detail vital negotiation groundworks (Michigan Association of School Boards, 2018). Chapter 2 will thoroughly discuss cost-containment tactics for group health benefits. For a precise district employment cost for an individual, complete figure 1.1.

Salary	________
Insurance (Single Plan-$15,000, Family Plan-$20,000)	________
Retirement (14% of Your Salary)	________
Social Security if Offered (6.2% of Your Salary)	________
Medicare (1.45% of Your Salary)	________
Workers' Compensation (1% of Your Salary)	________
Sick and Personal Leave (Add $3,000 on Average)	________
Tuition Assistance, if Applicable	________
In-Service Training (Meals, Travel, Lodging)	________
Other Benefits	________
Grand Total	________

Figure 1.1 Employee Cost

PURCHASING PROCEDURES

Maintaining proper purchasing practices safeguards legal procedures and sustains quality procurement internal controls. Although procedures governing purchasing may differ from district to district in the United States, the subsequent approach describes a model purchasing cycle. The superintendent in most districts across the country serves as the district purchasing agent.

In line with state legalities and adopted school policies, the superintendent oversees and administers the procurement program.

When an individual identifies the need for a resource and consults the administration or a colleague on the feasibility of buying a resource, the purchasing process commences. After concurrence to proceed, the purchaser and/or supervisor should analyze resource reviews to validate the best-valued product.

The person requesting the purchase in some districts completes a requisition and submits the form to the principal or supervisor for initial approval. The requested item, on occasion, must be purchased from a vendor on the state and/or district sanctioned list. Upon requisition form approval, the principal, supervisor, or business office employee enters the purchase requisition into the purchasing system (Shoop, 2019).

The district, by law, must purchase items only via properly approved purchase orders with sequential numbers. An authorized purchase order defines a legal contract that protects the school district and vendor during and after a purchase. The purchase order formally encumbers (i.e., sets aside) the funds by a line-item appropriation and lists the specific items, purchasing terms, and transaction conditions (Shoop, 2019).

Once authorized by each party in the approval chain (i.e., principal, supervisor, superintendent or designee, and CFO/treasurer), the assigned business office employee forwards the purchase order to the vendor and starts tracking the purchase. After receipt of the acquisition, the requisitioner or an appointed designee initials approval of the purchase in meeting the stipulated purchase order criteria (i.e., condition, quantity, and quality).

Upon satisfactory acceptance, the requisitioner or a designee sends a copy of the purchase order and signed packing slip to the purchasing office. The assigned business office employee then validates the purchase order against the packing slip and issues the final payment, which signifies purchase order fulfillment (Shoop, 2019).

Given the accessibility of computer technologies and integrated software today, a district may institute electronic purchasing, which automates and streamlines the acquisition process to save time and money. Computerized systems allow the staff to input requisitions and purchase orders, track purchase orders and invoices, record receipts, and issue vendor payments (Biedron, 2018a).

Proficient purchasing depicts obtaining the best-valued resource with the lowest price at the right time for the proper location. In order to ensure accurate processes, each staff member must realize their responsibilities. Table 1.1 shows recommended purchasing duty assignments by district size.

A school district may occasionally purchase assets from the same vendor on a reoccurring basis. A blanket purchase order (i.e., open purchase order)

Table 1.1 Recommended Purchasing Duty Assignments by District Size

Function	*Small District*	*Medium-Sized District*	*Large District*
Supervises the entire district purchasing functions	Superintendent	• Superintendent, • Purchasing Agent, or • Business Manager	Purchasing Administrator
Supervises district resource acquisition	Superintendent	Purchasing Agent	Purchasing Administrator
Assists in developing/modifying purchasing policies and procedures	• Superintendent and • CFO/Treasurer	• Superintendent, • CFO/Treasurer, and • Purchasing Agent	• Superintendent, • CFO/Treasurer, and • Purchasing Administrator
Approves all purchasing policies	School Board	School Board	School Board
Stays current on purchasing laws, regulations, and practices	• Administrators, • Superintendent, and • CFO/Treasurer	• Administrators, • Purchasing Agent, • Superintendent, and • CFO/Treasurer	• Administrators, • Purchasing Administrator, • Superintendent, and CFO/Treasurer
Supervises building/department resource acquisition	• Principal or • Supervisor	• Principal, • Assistant Principal, or • Supervisor	• Principal, • Assistant Principal, or • Supervisor
Initiates purchase orders	Designated Personnel	Designated Personnel	Designated Personnel
Creates purchase orders	• Designated Personnel or • CFO/Treasurer	• Designated Personnel, • CFO/Treasurer, or • Clerical Support Designee	• Designated Personnel or • Clerical Support Designee
Assigns purchase order numbers	• Business Office Designee or • CFO/Treasurer	• Business Office Designee or • CFO/Treasurer	Business Office Designee
Authorizes all purchase orders	• Superintendent and • CFO/Treasurer	• Purchasing Agent and • CFO/Treasurer	• Purchasing Administrator and • CFO/Treasurer
Contacts vendors and maintains purchase order files	Business Office Designee	Business Office Designee	Business Office Designee
Distributes resources to user	Clerical Support Designee	Clerical Support Designee	Clerical Support Designee
Checks resources against the purchase order and signs the packing slip to signify a completed purchase	• Requesting Employee, • Clerical Support Designee, or • Designated Administrator	• Requesting Employee, • Clerical Support Designee, or • Designated Administrator	• Requesting Employee, • Clerical Support Designee, or • Designated Administrator
Validates resources against the purchase order and packing slip to verify a completed purchase order	Business Office Designee	Business Office Designee	Clerical Support Designee
Authorizes purchase order payment	CFO/Treasurer	Business Office Designee	Business Office Designee

authorizes multiple purchases at different times on a single purchase order to the same vendor for a specified time frame. A blanket purchase order eliminates repetitive data entry, increases efficiency, and remains legal as long as the total expenditures do not exceed a minimal percentage of the sum. School districts in most states and the District of Columbia (i.e., jurisdictions) may sanction a more restrictive blanket purchasing policy than mandated by law; however, board policy may not be less restrictive than the law (Texas Education Agency, 2019b).

An after-the-fact purchase occurs when a purchaser accepts a resource prior to the issuance of an authorized purchase order. State laws and board policies differ in ways to deal with an after-the-fact purchase.

A district purchase, without prior approval, is an unauthorized commitment of funds in most instances. As such, the transaction is illegal and may result in an audit finding against the district, especially when school officials do not properly identify the illegal transaction and immediately resolve the issue. The individual who initiates an unlawful purchase may be held personally responsible for payment, notified about the unauthorized act, subjected to criminal prosecution, and/or disciplined by school district personnel. An after-the-fact purchase order in Ohio may become legal, when the school board passes a resolution to approve a "Then and Now Certificate" (Ohio Auditor Office, 2018).

In another instance, a memorandum from the Assistant Superintendent for Business and Finance at the Phoenix Union High School District in Arizona notified employees about a three-strike system for after-the-fact purchases. With a first offense, a business office official contacts the individual who commits the purchasing violation and that employee's supervisor. The offender must complete a form to acknowledge the problem payment. This first warning commands the supervisor to discuss proper purchasing procedures with the offending individual, and the business office staff member authorizes payment upon consenting signatures (McCleery, 2019).

When an individual has a second after-the-fact purchase at the Phoenix Union High School District, the violator and supervisor follow the same routine as a first instance with payment by the district, but school officials may discipline the wrongdoer. Upon notice of a third violation by the same person, the lawbreaker and principal must appear before the board of education to respond to the incident. The board of education trustees then decide who will pay the vendor—the district, offender, and/or principal. A third violation may result in termination and a felony indictment (McCleery, 2019).

COST-EFFICIENT PROCUREMENT PRACTICES

To efficiently manage school district resources, school administrators must proficiently perform a variety of procurement practices by employing contract and price negotiations; bulk acquisitions; supply warehouses; product standardization; pilots; equipment leases; open educational supplies; outsourced services; centralized, cooperative, and credit card purchases; and surplus, obsolete, or unused resource disposals.

Accomplished school administrators with skillful contract negotiation skills save districts thousands of dollars by bargaining lower resource prices than the cataloged cost. The ability to negotiate purchase charges and terms proficiently exemplifies a crucial school leadership skill.

Administrators, too often, recommend or purchase resources without planning or bargaining prices. School officials will broker purchases more effectively through early identification of essential products, imminent contract renewals, and potential new contracts. After identification, school officials should prioritize each purchase by dollar, vendor, and/or degree of negotiation complexity. Armed with a calendar of future purchases, school administrators communicate expectations, define necessary outcomes, and negotiate transactions better than without purchasing data (Shell, 2019).

Buying resources in large quantities denotes another strategy to save district money, reduces management time, and portrays smooth deliveries. To implement bulk purchasing, school leaders must possess an awareness of resource needs and a command of efficient business office procedures. When administrators lack these capacities, bulk purchasing could result in needless inventories, cramped storage spaces, and impulse buys. Although few standard rules subsist for bulk purchasing, a familiarity with staff needs and an understanding of necessary resources shape the most prolific routines (Brimley et al., 2020).

Because many states maintain statewide systems to buy products in bulk and arrange to offer districts' savings on particular supplies and equipment, centralized purchasing agreements and competitive bid contracts from the state may be advantageous for schools. Centralized purchasing, as a complement to bulk purchasing, depicts a purchasing system that concentrates the authority, responsibility, and control of purchasing activities to one administrative unit (Brimley et al., 2020).

Centralized purchasing at the district level generally combines purchases for common needs with two or more schools. Districts that employ centralized purchasing tactics normally sustain a greater capacity to manage contracts and resolve disputes, maintain superior records and product evaluations, augment meaningful support training, and negotiate costs and terms better than decentralized purchasing processes (Brimley et al., 2020).

Centralized purchasing makes definite sense when purchasing employee group health insurance. On the other hand, a decentralized purchasing system with decisions at the school level may match end user needs better than centralized purchasing. End users, within decentralized processes, easily admit purchase outcomes, typically limit bad effects, ordinarily simplify bureaucracy, and frequently quicken delivery times. End users and vendors, further, may communicate better in decentralized purchasing than centralized purchasing (Biedron, 2018b). School districts should ultimately employ an appropriate mix of centralized and decentralized purchasing strategies based on needs and capacities (Brimley et al., 2020).

Supplies or materials have little value when they are unavailable as needed; therefore, inventory storage becomes a consideration. Centralized storage may lead to tighter district control and heightened accountability by reducing the number of employees in the custody chain. Storage at the building level, on the contrary, usually triggers quicker material accessibility and closer local control than central storage, although less experienced staff may handle supplies at the building. Food and perishable commodities assuredly necessitate special storage conditions (Brimley et al., 2020). Based on needs and space, a combination of centralized and local inventory storage will prove beneficial for a district and school.

Standardization of materials, supplies, and equipment may save the district money by reducing inventories and decreasing expensive repairs. When a district standardizes purchasing school buses and warehouses similar inoperable manufacturer's makes, the district may cannibalize parts from broken buses for repairs, which may lower costs. When declaring standards for standardized purchasing, school administrators, however, may be tempted to buy an ill-advised product, causing unwise expenditures or poor execution. School officials, however, must be aware of competitive bid law and not violate the law in standardizing products. As a negative, standardization implies additional time and effort in preparing specifications than without normalization (Brimley et al., 2020).

Piloting a resource (e.g., textbook or software) before purchasing distinguishes another worthwhile strategy to secure quality assets. A pilot refers to a partnership between a vendor and a school district, when the district uses the resources for an extended time (i.e., school year) without purchasing the item. A pilot typically differs from a free short-term trial because usage in a pilot remains for an extended time. Before participating in a pilot, school officials should plan detailed logistics; question the vendor about the agreement; and dedicate time, support, and planning for professional development (Slutsky, 2017).

To execute an efficacious pilot, a district must set specific goals (e.g., acquire a textbook series or software) and verify participants (e.g., teachers willing to implement the resources). A district with a pilot should define a sufficient participation time (e.g., one full school year), invest in professional development, arrange a planned conclusion (e.g., resource evaluation), and be transparent with interested parties—vendors, administrators, staff, and parents (Slutsky, 2017). Pilots have been particularly advantageous in software and textbook acquisitions.

Leasing equipment, particularly for technology hardware (e.g., laptops, tablets, servers, desktops, printers, whiteboards, projectors, and copiers), constitutes an alternative to the traditional approach of purchasing technology. Avoiding up-front costs, conserving dollars, and instituting consistent payments are benefits of renting resources. By leasing products, a district may offer state-of-the-art technology to the students and staff. A renewed lease typically affords the district with the most current resource. Leasing technology equipment also supports socioeconomic equality by guaranteeing that all students access the same devices (Hamilton, n.d.).

In some lease undertakings, the district becomes the owner after the lease expires. High borrowing interest rates charged by vendors, inexplicable leasing terms and conditions, and hidden fees at the lease's conclusion exemplify drawbacks to renting equipment. To enlist a profitable leasing program, school leaders must completely understand the agreement terms, conditions, and district obligations; skillfully compare multiple vendors' costs (e.g., interest rates and expenses for training, maintenance, support, and disposal); and thoughtfully evaluate the rental options, even though a price quotation may not be mandated (Hamilton, n.d.).

Encouraging and utilizing open educational resources (OERs) illustrate another potential cost savings for school districts. OERs to support student learning may encompass course materials, lesson plans, textbooks, content videos, tests, and software. Open sources represent public domain and Creative Commons materials that permit free use and/or repurpose by staff and students. By remixing, modifying, or redistributing OER materials, the sources become flexible in terms of customizing and sharing with others (Lynch, 2019).

Districts that employ OERs usually shift budgeted dollars spent on textbooks and materials to other educational priorities. OER content with regular updates will save the district money and remain more current than printed material. Overcoming staff resistance to change and the length of time to vet materials epitomize the biggest challenges in OER implementation (Lynch, 2019).

Outsourcing or privatizing services attempts to reduce district budgets or improve production by hiring a private enterprise to manage and perform a district's auxiliary service—transportation, cafeteria operation, custodial and maintenance, security, or technology repair.

According to outsourcing proponents, a district's primary job is to educate children; consequently, districts should privatize any task detracting from that mission. Outsourcing, with this in mind, may be a less expensive proposition than the district employing the workforce. The contracted company may offer lower wages to employees than the district's negotiated agreement. A district, additionally, will not be paying for employee benefits. Further, due in part to economies of scale, a firm that specializes in a particular service may buy necessary supplies in bulk at discounted rates (Andersson, Jordahl, & Josephson, 2019).

Critics, to the contrary, claim that outsourcing a service restricts district control, displaces existing workers, increases disbursements in subsequent contracts, and simply does not perform the work as proficiently as the district staff who most often care about the community, school, and student body (Andersson et al., 2019).

Before outsource implementation, administrators should analyze the reasons for outsourcing. Beyond cost savings, administrators should exercise due diligence by carefully contemplating privatization's social impact on the community workforce, public relations, and staff morale. The loss of district management control, the time to manage the privatized contract, and lack of flexibility epitomizes other considerations (Andersson et al., 2019).

In order to ensure well-executed outsourcing, the district must carefully review requests for bids, vendors' past performances, contract provisions, and cancellation clauses. Administrators should conduct a thorough, comparative analysis between an in-house and outsourced service by weighing the disadvantages and advantages for each arrangement. After a district privatization decision, the district should exhibit clear communications to those individuals directly impacted by the change to ensure a smooth transition (Andersson et al., 2019).

Cooperative purchasing, another form of outsourcing, connects a school district with other organizations to acquire resources via an interlocal agreement. To become a cooperative member, a district's board of education approves a resolution granting the district permission to participate in membership and authorizes accompanying fees. A school district with this association may purchase materials, supplies, buses, equipment, or services through the cooperative. In many states, mandated competitive bidding by a cooperative agency may replace the district's bid requirement.

According to the National Association of State Procurement Officials (2019), cooperative purchasing agreements

- offer better prices to participating schools and advanced negotiating power due to aggregated economies of scale than lone district purchasing;
- secure first-rate resources because the cooperative personnel may dedicate more time to research, verify, and evaluate products than the district staff;
- deliver superior technical expertise;
- identify, control, and standardize resource specifications; and

- save administrative time because the cooperative staff develops, receives, assesses, and selects competitive bids when necessary.

Cooperative purchasing, however, is not without challenges. Specifications, terms, and conditions must be reconciled before finalizing a vendor contract. Cooperative purchasing, at the earliest inception, solely entailed buying cleaning supplies and paper; however, cooperative arrangements incorporate many items today (National Association of State Procurement Officials, 2019; Texas Association of School Boards, 2019).

School districts may employ cooperative provisions to purchase information technology services, propane fuel, computer hardware, electronic defibrillators, wireless radios, cell phones, and fleet vehicles. As a concern with cooperative purchasing, schools may not be able to support a neighborhood business because of the group accord. In spite of the difficulties, a district benefits from cooperative purchasing due to lower prices, better resource applications, and more efficient operations than lone district purchasing (National Association of State Procurement Officials, 2019; Texas Association of School Boards, 2019).

Purchasing cards (i.e., p-cards) allow school districts to issue electronic payments for expenses, such as conference lodging, gasoline, or office supplies. Similar to a consumer credit card, accountable staff members may employ p-cards for acquisitions. Because online purchasing may be coordinated with a purchasing card, p-cards streamline the procurement-to-payment process and allow schools to acquire goods and services in a timelier, more cost-effective manner than customary purchasing. Reducing transaction costs, tracking disbursements faster, leveraging discount buying, and deemphasizing the need for petty cash remain p-card advantages over conventional purchasing. Many p-card programs offer rebates to school districts based on annual spending, which is a benefit for switching to p-cards. The key to success is getting p-cards into the hands of trustworthy staff members who are currently making small purchases that generate purchase orders of less than $1,000 (Texas Education Agency, 2019b).

Well-defined procedures for the disposal of surplus, obsolete, or unused assets may be financially beneficial to a district. In accordance with state law or school board policy, the district may dispose of district real and tangible property within dollar limitations. Alternative methods for disposal may include donating the items to state and local agencies; trading the objects for useful resources; or selling the resources through consignments, online means, or public auctions. When objects owned by the school have little value, as a last resort, the district may offer the items to a salvage dealer or recycling center (Ohio School Boards Association, 2018b).

The disposal of surplus and obsolete tangible property by public auction may be effective, when organized properly. District officials should compile the sales list of auctioned items, including the description (make/model), serial number, district tag number, and quantity. The school board should approve the selling list before the sale.

When required by district policy, school leaders should establish a minimum bid, advertise the public auction well in advance of the event, and extensively distribute the notice. Nonprofit organizations and nonpublic schools in some states must be given the opportunity to view and purchase the items before a public sale. The district should arrange for a satisfactory auction location and decide who will conduct the auction—professional auctioneer, community member, or staff associate (Ohio School Boards Association, 2018b). To properly dispose of surplus, obsolete, or unused assets, school officials should review board policy and/or state law.

When an eligible party does not accept an offer within 60 days, the board may dispose of the property by public auction (i.e., items valued more than $10,000) or by private sale (i.e., items valued less than $10,000). When arranging a public auction, the board must distribute a written notice in a newspaper of general circulation at least 30 days before the auction or post a notice at five public locations within the school district (Ohio School Boards Association, 2018b). State law; board policy; community mindset; space to sort, price, and store the contents; and the necessary planning time to prepare for a sale are disposal considerations.

PRICE QUOTATIONS AND COMPETITIVE BIDS

School administrators face a number of decisions when considering a purchase. Identifying the need and researching possible solutions to satisfy the need mark the initial steps. Based on the estimated purchase price, the superintendent or designee may employ a purchase order, price quotation, request for bid, competitive, or sealed bid because procurement adheres to strict observance of associated state statutes (see table 1.2), board policies, and regulations regarding each type of action.

Some states or school boards may mandate that districts acquire a price quotation in lieu of competitive bidding, when purchases cost below a certain dollar threshold. Price quotes dictated by state law hold varying threshold levels and procedural prerequisites. School boards may enact stricter local policy for price quotations than state law requirements.

A price quote aims to ascertain the lowest, reasonable price on less expensive resources, thereby creating competition among vendors. A price quote exhibits less time and administrative effort than a sealed bid because detailed instructions and descriptive qualifications are not compulsory. Written specifications, however, are beneficial to compare exact quotes. School officials should summon quotes from known as well as interested suppliers and accept quotations in person or by electronic mail, facsimile, phone call, or postal mail. Written responses express the best documentation.

To begin a price quote, the administrator or staff member typically clarifies purchasing fundamentals, solicits quotes from qualified suppliers on the local or state vendor eligibility list, compares price quotes, and identifies the least expensive item from the most responsible vendor who offers the best resource. Upon quote selection, the designated employee issues a purchase order. The school board frequently remains uninvolved in the process to award purchases from quotations (New Jersey Association of School Business Officials, 2018).

Based on the estimated resource cost, a number of states permit or encourage districts to purchase resources utilizing a request for bid (i.e., proposal). A request for bid signifies a procurement method that exceeds price quote obligations but falls short of competitive sealed bid commitments. Based on related state law or board policy, a request for bid may involve public advertising and submitting notices to potential vendors. A request for bid does not always include specific product descriptions; purchasing via a request for bid allows suppliers to meet general expectations and submit proposals with their own specifications (New Jersey Association of School Business Officials, 2018).

With a request for bid, school district personnel stay unobligated to select the lowest proposal; the district staff may evaluate the offers based upon the district's needs. Because vendors usually present dissimilar resources of differing value, the best price and value remain challenging to ascertain. After accepting requests for bid, staff members may modify stipulations and renegotiate the proposal's terms, conditions, and prices with one or more bidders. School officers may open proposals at any time and in any manner. The school board may participate in awarding this type of bid (New Jersey Association of School Business Officials, 2018).

Competitive bidding characterizes a formal process mandated by state law, when individuals or firms submit competitive bids to supply a resource to government agencies, including school districts. Procurement law for each state generally contains minimum cost thresholds for competitive bidding with advertising regulations, bid bond directives, emergency procurement exceptions, and procedures to award and reject bids. Contract law principles (i.e., offer and acceptance) apply to agreements let under competitive bidding, and accepted competitive bids stand irrevocable (National Association of State Procurement Officials, 2019; New Jersey Association of School Business Officials, 2018).

Competitive bidding creates an open, fair, and transparent business atmosphere, meaning that any company may submit a bid regardless of its size, capital, or other factors. Districts should welcome all bids for a resource and grant businesses a fair chance to earn the bid in open competition (National Association of State Procurement Officials, 2019).

A sealed competitive bid, often directed by state law, derived from the offline world with bids independently submitted in sealed envelopes, securely stored in a named location, openly viewed at a public forum, and publicly announced at a specified time, date, and place. This purchasing approach ensures that the school district does not interfere with the bids or steer the selection. School district personnel, with competitive bidding, cannot share bid offers in advance of the official opening date or permit an enterprise to adjust a bid after the final submission deadline (National Association of State Procurement Officials, 2019).

Web applications in today's world facilitate an electronic version of the sealed bid. Bidders submit bids as form entries, attach documents through a secure login on the application, and edit the bid anytime until the submission deadline. An electronic signature authorizes bids. By electronically submitting a bid, the technology tools safeguard the school management's integrity throughout the process and deliver a centralized, collaborative workspace for viewing and evaluating bids (National Association of State Procurement Officials, 2019).

With mandatory competitive bidding, state statutes and board policies also direct the general steps for electronic and nonelectronic bidding processes. After recognizing that the purchase warrants competitive bidding, the superintendent should garner approval from the school board to advertise for bids and prepare supplementary documents.

A public notice or newspaper advertisement may solicit and publicize the invitation for bids within a reasonable time prior to the bid opening. The invitation for bids contains all the bid documents for executing a bid, such as the acquisition descriptions or specifications; proposed contract terms and conditions; bid opening time, date, and place; evaluative criteria for offers; and the need for a bid guaranty (National Association of State Procurement Officials, 2019; New Jersey Association of School Business Officials, 2018).

A bid guaranty assures that the winning bidder will fulfill the contract as bid after district selection and bidder acceptance. When a bidder fails to fulfill a contract, the company forfeits the surety. Cash, certified check, or surety bond (e.g., bid bond) payable to the district constitutes forms of bid guaranty (i.e., 5% of the bid amount). A performance bond (i.e., 25% of contract amount) refers to an insurance agreement where a third-party insurer accepts liability in the event that a company defaults in successfully fulfilling the bid conditions (Abrahams & Motz, 2019).

Before the bid opening, a school district may host a prebid conference to answer questions for prospective bidders. The district staff may also prequalify bidders by examining potential bidders' financial ability to satisfy a contract and assessing bidders' experiences in successfully completing similar bids (National Association of State Procurement Officials, 2019).

Districts, in accordance with competitive bid statutes, must publicly open all sealed bids at the designated time, date, and location. The district, thereby, accepts the bids without alterations or corrections. Interested parties, school board members, and the public may be present to witness the bid opening and delineations. District personnel records basic bid information and permits public inspection (Abrahams & Motz, 2019; Alexander & Alexander, 2019).

When a bid does not substantially conform to the instructions, the district's school board may reject the bid. District personnel, at the bid opening, do not have to decide the lowest, responsible bid. The lowest, responsible bid describes an offer from a responsible bidder who proposes a bid in compliance with all the terms and conditions of the invitation for bids; offers the lowest bid price; and delivers the best reputation, experience, financial capability, and historical performance to fulfill the contract (Alexander & Alexander, 2019).

A three- to six-member evaluation committee should confer at a bid evaluation meeting in order to prioritize the bids and select the lowest, responsible bidder (National Association of State Procurement Officials, 2019). The following variables may determine the lowest, responsible bidder:

- price;
- company financial capacity;
- vendor reputation for honest, reliable work;
- expertise in performing the proposed bid;
- accessible repair parts; and
- past performances, including service (National Association of State Procurement Officials, 2019).

Upon selecting the lowest, responsible bid, the superintendent or designee recommends the proposed winning bidder to the board of education for approval. After the board of education affirmatively votes to award the bid, the contract is absolute and binding. The superintendent or designee then notifies the successful and unsuccessful bidders. When a school district fails to comply with the procurement statute regulations in any way, the contract is void and unenforceable, and district personnel must begin the bidding process from the start, when still wanting to obtain the resource.

After board approval and acceptance by the lowest, responsible bidder, a district designee generates a purchase order for the contract and monitors the purchase/bid developments; a district administrator or designee must return the guaranties to the unsuccessful bidders in a reasonable time. With a fulfilled contract, a final inspection follows. When the resource meets contractual requirements, a district staff member authorizes acceptance; the vendor then receives payment (National Association of State Procurement Officials, 2019).

Statutory regulations in many states often address exceptions to competitive bid law. When a district confirms a public emergency, demands a special skill, specifies a unique item, verifies a sole provider, or purchases a utility service, state procurement law generally exempts the district from competitive bid regulations (National Association of State Procurement Officials, 2019).

In the case of an emergency that warrants urgent attention in Ohio, for instance, a school district may forgo competitive bid stipulations in order to remedy the circumstance. The school board, by resolution, declares that the situation presents an "urgent necessity" due to possible serious harm to district property or an individual's health and safety (Ohio School Boards Association, 2018a).

Procurement law in most states excuses districts from competitive bid obligations in contracts with insurance companies, accountants, attorneys, auditors, and others who offer personal services that necessitate a special skill. As a rationale for this exception, courts have found that the lowest bidder may underbid more experienced individuals, causing the district to accept inferior services (Ohio School Boards Association, 2018a).

Districts in many states may purchase unique items without competitive bidding, such as textbooks, instructional materials, or computer software because the quality of these teaching resources is critical to student learning. Subsequent laws often declare that districts must not abide by the lowest bidder standard for these items (Beardsley et al., 2017).

When a single source remains the only viable option to purchase an item, competitive bidding is fruitless. A board resolution in this event, thereby, identifies this solitary purchasing source. Public utilities (e.g., water, gas, and electricity) generally do not command competitive bid protocols because only a single company may serve the area (Texas Education Agency, 2019b).

All states and the District of Columbia have formal protest mechanisms within statutes in case of a suspected competitive bid violation. A bidder or interested party adversely affected in connection with a bid solicitation, award, or contract administration may file a complaint; however, the definition of objections, filing prerequisites, hearing officer's duties, and response times vary by state (National Association of State Procurement Officials, 2019).

As a best practice, Alaska, California, Delaware, Hawaii, Iowa, Massachusetts, Michigan, New York, Pennsylvania, and the District of Columbia have a mandatory debriefing session after a bid opening. Debriefings, as an informational tool, grant vendors feedback on their specific proposal, identifying strengths and weaknesses. Florida, Hawaii, Nevada, South Carolina, and Tennessee stipulate a bond with a complaint submission (National Association of State Procurement Officials, 2019). After identifying a purchase need, the superintendent and/or designee must realize when the district should legally employ a price quotation, request for proposal, competitive, or sealed bid.

Jurisdiction (i.e., states and the District of Columbia) procurement law typically presents directives and threshold levels for price quotations, requests for bids, and sealed competitive bids. Under special circumstances, the purchase may be exempt from state procurement law, although the projected price exceeds legal thresholds. After reviewing jurisdiction procurement laws, the superintendent or designee must properly select the precise solicitation method (New Jersey Association of School Business Officials, 2018). To review a particular jurisdiction's procurement laws, regulations, and policies, click or search for the Appendix of National Association of State Procurement Officials [2018] *Survey of State Procurement Practices* at https://www.naspo.org/Portals/16/2018%20Survey/2018%20FINAL%20Survey%20Report_6-14-18.pdf.

PROCUREMENT AT NONPUBLIC AND PUBLIC CHARTER SCHOOLS

Nonpublic Schools

Nonpublic schools across the country, administered by a variety of governance models, hold much latitude in developing operational policies and practices regarding procurement. Governance authority in Catholic schools, for instance, have one of the three versions—local pastor or canonical administrator, bishop or designee (e.g., diocesan office staff), or board (Calkins & Convey, 2019).

Because canon law allows ecclesial officials to delegate responsibilities at their discretion, board configurations may be advisory, consultative, limited, or absolute. As such, governance versions may be executive in nature with a dedicated local or central office staff member responsible for approving policies or collegial at the local and central office level with policy development tasks shared among individuals (Calkins & Convey, 2019).

Regardless of the governance model, nonpublic schools may elect to employ any desired procedures regarding procurement or purchasing because state law does not limit their actions in the same manner as public entities. To guarantee that nonpublic schools astutely spend dollars with market-driven prices, nonpublic school administrators, nonetheless, should implement the cost-efficient practices from this chapter to receive the best price for purchased resources, including the processes for price quotation solicitations, requests for bids, competitive, or sealed bids.

Public Charter Schools

Freedom from rules and regulations, including procurement, highlights a public charter school hallmark across the nation. A majority of states and the District of Columbia grant significant freedom from laws and regulations to public charter schools. Four states (see table 1.2) do not allow any state law exemptions, including competitive bid procedures.

The charter school authorizer in 14 states may request an exemption from state laws. Charter school law in Alabama automatically exempts charter schools from most state laws; however, the state's charter proviso stipulates that charter schools must comply with competitive bid laws. Twenty-six states and the District of Columbia offer automatic waivers from regulations, excluding federal statutes and jurisdiction laws pertaining to health, safety, civil rights, student accountability, employee criminal background checks, open meetings, freedom of information, and generally accepted accounting principles. Six states do not permit charter schools (Education Commission of the States, 2018a; National Alliance for Public Charter Schools, 2019). Table 1.2 shows law exemptions for public charter schools by jurisdiction.

Although some states compel charter schools to submit budgets, report fiscal data utilizing generally accepted accounting principles, and conduct independent financial audits, many states relieve charter schools from best procurement practices. Charter schools, nonetheless, may sanction business actions in their charter policy and elect to utilize price quotations, requests for bids, competitive, or sealed bids to receive the best price for purchased resources.

Taxpayers have invested $40 billion in charter schools across the country since the first inception by Minnesota in 1991. Local, state, and federal governmental bodies that oversee and finance charter schools, however, have failed to protect, monitor, and ensure that these monies benefit communities and students. Passive oversight systems remain reactive, while whistleblowers, reporters, and investigators must notify state auditors about suspected abuses at charter schools (Center for Popular Democracy, 2017).

Table 1.2 Charter School Law Exemptions[a]

Jurisdiction	*State Laws Not Waived*	*May Apply for Exemption*	*Automatic Waivers*	*Jurisdiction*	*State Laws Not Waived*	*May Apply for Exemption*	*Automatic Waivers*
Alabama[b]			X	Mississippi			X
Alaska		X		Missouri			X
Arizona			X	Nevada		X	
Arkansas		X		New Hampshire			X
California			X	New Jersey		X	
Colorado			X	New Mexico		X	
Connecticut		X		New York			X
Delaware		X		North Carolina			X
Florida			X	Ohio			X
Georgia		X		Oklahoma			X
Hawaii			X	Oregon			X
Idaho			X	Pennsylvania	X		
Illinois			X	Rhode Island		X	
Indiana			X	South Carolina			X
Iowa			X	Tennessee		X	
Kansas		X		Texas			X
Kentucky			X	Utah		X	
Louisiana			X	Virginia		X	
Maine			X	Washington			X
Maryland		X		Washington, DC			X
Massachusetts	X			Wisconsin			X
Michigan	X			Wyoming	X		
Minnesota			X	Total	4	14	27

Notes: [a]The table does not list Montana, Nebraska, North Dakota, South Dakota, Vermont, and West Virginia because these states have not passed a charter school law.

[b]Alabama does not exclude public charter schools from competitive bid law, although the state waives other laws.

Sources: Education Commission of the States (2018a) and National Alliance for Public Charter Schools (2019).

The Center for Popular Democracy (2017) further revealed that charter schools in 15 states have mismanaged over $223 million since 1994. This report verified cases of fraud, waste, and abuse due to inadequate internal controls over basic fiscal operations, a lack of proper procurement procedures (i.e., competitive bidding), as well as inconsistent or improper purchasing processes.

As stated by the Center for Popular Democracy (2017), charter schools should be subject to the same financial transparency and accountability as applied to each state's public school. A jurisdiction's charter school law should address financial conflicts of interest and misappropriation of public funds by charter school officials or administrators who personally gain by malfeasances. To ensure accountability, jurisdiction charter law should order charter schools across the country to commission an annual audit with quality internal controls.

SUMMARY

School districts have limited dollars for spending; thus, there is only "so much pie" (i.e., money). Districts must employ efficient, lawful procedures for district resource procurement. School administrators and board members must recognize and implement superlative business practices to ensure that the district spends an appropriate amount of school money on classroom instruction to "get the most bang for the buck." In accordance with national, state, and local purchasing procurement laws and regulations, a fiscally responsible school district should have management processes in place to purchase resources from the right source, for the right quantity, with the right quality, and at the right price.

Strategic planning, a noteworthy management activity, causes a district to define its goals and objectives, establish priorities, and solidify specific tactics to achieve the school's mission. Although many districts engage in planning focused on improving instruction, fiscally responsible districts link both strategic and improvement plans to resource allocation for achieving and supporting instructional goals (National Association of State Procurement Officials, 2019).

Because employees' salaries and benefits comprise a large percentage of a district's budget, fiscally responsible school district personnel should clearly aim to manage these expenses effectively. While overseeing personnel expenses, school boards and administrators overwhelmingly desire to offer the staff competitive wages and allowances that permit districts to recruit, reward, and retain the best and brightest employees.

A variety of business practices emphasize actions to save a school district money—acquiring acquisitions in bulk; warehousing supplies in centralized locations; leasing, standardizing, and piloting resources; utilizing OERs; outsourcing services; studying centralized versus decentralized purchasing; employing consortiums and credit card methods; and disposing of surplus, obsolete, or unused equipment and materials. Price negotiating via quotations, requests for bids, competitive, and sealed bids facilitate the potential acquisition of the lowest, responsible values for particular resources.

Employing business procedures with technology solutions that promote agile procurement, price competition, and ethical principles with fair and transparent processes will set a district on the course for efficient, accountable resource management (National Association of State Procurement Officials, 2019).

PROJECTS

1. Using figure 1.1, calculate the cost of your employment.
2. Investigate and report the purchasing policies and procedures for your district, including blanket purchase orders, e-purchases, and after-the-fact situations.
3. Examine and relate the various purchasing duties (see table 1.1) by job title in your district.
4. Locate and analyze a district's procurement or purchasing manual in light of the chapter content.
5. Identify and record the cost-efficient procurement practices employed by your district and recommend underutilized practices that could yield cost savings.
6. Research and describe your jurisdiction's price quotation and competitive bid laws (see the appendix in the *Survey of State Procurement Practices* at https://www.naspo.org/Portals/16/2018%20Survey/2018%20FINAL%20Survey%20Report_6-14-18.pdf).
7. Observe and document a price quote or request for bid in your school district.
8. Inspect and report a competitive or sealed bid executed by your school, including the supplementary documentation (e.g., advertisement, instructions, specifications, and evaluation criteria).
9. Research, observe, and document the process for a district's active competitive or sealed bid or discover the plans for a future bid.
10. Under the direct guidance of a school superintendent or architect, develop and execute a competitive or sealed bid, including the written advertisement, bid instructions, specifications, and evaluation criteria.

Chapter 2

Employee Benefits and Risk Management

OBJECTIVES

After reading this chapter, you should be able to

- ✓ critique your district's employee health insurance plan document, identify coverages, classify cost-sharing provisions, and compare findings with another district's plan (NELP 5.3, 6.1, 6.2, 6.3, 7.3, 7.4);
- ✓ analyze a district's insurance utilization data and devise provisions for district/employee cost savings (NELP 5.3, 6.1, 6.2, 6.3, 7.3, 7.4);
- ✓ articulate current healthcare issues at the local, jurisdiction, and national levels (NELP 6.1, 6.2, 7.3, 7.4); and
- ✓ distinguish principles in pension assurances plus professional liability, unemployment, workers' compensation, property, general liability, and fleet insurances and detect opportunities to save money for a district in each program (NELP 5.3, 6.1, 6.2, 7.3, 7.4).

A century ago, benefits granted by employers to employees were uncommon. Today, by contrast, employee benefits (i.e., fringe benefits) for educators and other workers represent a significant compensation component, albeit nonsalary in most cases. Medical, vision, dental, short- and long-term disabilities, and life insurances illustrate voluntarily offered employee benefits. Pension, unemployment insurance, workers' compensation, Medicare, paid leave from work, and professional liability protection characterize benefits mandated by state or federal law (Martocchio, 2018).

Additional fringe benefits tendered to certified and classified school employees may include in-service training (e.g., conference registration fees, meals, travel, and lodging) and tuition assistance. Superintendents and other high-ranking district administrators may collect benefits above staff allowances, including compensated professional membership fees; cell phone, computer, and vehicle loans; paid civic organization dues; vacation leave; and relocation costs (McCord & Finnan, 2019).

Benefit opportunities advanced over the years because school employers must compete against economic forces in the job market. Keeping benefit expenditures from crushing the school budget creates a challenge because these expenses dramatically outpaced the typical annual inflation rate. Riley, Schneiter, Hensley-Quinn, Cousart, and Horvath (2019) claimed that insurance premium costs for state-sponsored employee health plans increased more than 14% faster than those similar expenses for large, private sector firms. Sisko et al. (2019) projected annual national healthcare expenses to grow 5.5% annually from 2019 to 2027, representing faster growth than the economy.

Given the continued shortage of teachers, administrators, and support staff, schools must offer a substantial fringe benefit package and a competitive salary to attract and retain qualified personnel. Due to the effect that employee benefit expenditures hold on a district's budget, school administrators must be keenly aware of these allowances and related costs (Bruno, 2019).

As presented by Snyder, de Brey, and Dillow (2019), fringe benefit costs denoted a district's second-largest expenditure category after salaries during the 2017 fiscal year, which is the most current data available from U.S. Department of Education at the time of publication. These expenses across the nation averaged 23% of a district's entire operating budget. The U.S. Department of Labor (2019b) reported that the national teacher's salary averaged 66.5% of an employee's compensation package with total benefits equaling 33.5% during 2018. Insurances, countrywide, averaged 11.1% of the complete employee compensation package; retirement, 12.6%; paid leave, 4.7%; supplemental pay, 0.3%; and other legally required benefits, 4.8%.

State statutes, federal laws, and union contracts, when in force, shape benefit packages for school employees. States hold different collective bargaining laws related to benefits. In those states that permit bargaining, negotiations impact benefits, employee insurance plans, coverages, and costs.

Health insurance programs bargained collectively offered better benefits at a lower employee cost than nonunion plans, as reported by the U.S. Department of Labor (2019c) during the March 2019 period. Nationwide, 95% of all union members in governmental positions (i.e., state and local) accessed medical benefits, including primary and secondary educators, while only 68% of nonunion members accessed these benefits during the March 2019 reporting period (U.S. Department of Labor, 2019c).

Eighty-nine percent of employees at elementary and secondary schools had access to healthcare benefits during the March 2019 period. Seventy-five percent of primary and secondary school employees participated in group healthcare benefits (U.S. Department of Labor, 2019c).

The National Council on Teacher Quality (2019) recounted that fringe benefits were a mandatory subject of bargaining in 24 states and the District of Columbia (see table 2.1). Bargaining for fringe benefits was permissive in six states and not addressed in state law or administrative code in 13 states; seven states do not permit bargaining for fringe benefits.

Because most states administered pension programs, bargaining issue was not addressed in 21 states. School boards in Florida, Indiana, Kansas, Massachusetts, Michigan, Missouri, Ohio, Oregon, Pennsylvania, and Wisconsin must bargain pension benefits. Arkansas, Colorado, Maine, Minnesota, and the District of Columbia have permissive laws for bargaining retirement benefits. Connecticut, Iowa, New Jersey, New York, and Tennessee prohibit collective bargaining for pension benefits (National Council on Teacher Quality, 2019).

With the escalation of benefit expenses, school superintendents, in particular, should be especially knowledgeable about cost-containment measures. When these expenses negatively impact the school budget in dramatic ways, the superintendent is typically held the most accountable. Superintendents should expressly note that spiraling fringe benefit costs are not solely the board of education or chief financial officer's concerns. School officials, too often, believe these costs are out of their control, but this belief is inaccurate in many cases. By understanding the way insurances function, the district staff and administrators may uncover cost savings through an inclusive, dedicated effort.

EMPLOYEE BENEFITS

Paid Leaves

Paid leave, the most common district-offered benefit, compensates employees for approved work breaks. School districts typically extend paid leave for illness, injury, personal reasons, vacations, holidays, bereavement, jury duty, and military service. State law often stipulates the specific number of days and conditions for sick and personal leaves, whereas federal laws regulate military leave and protect employees and/or families in distinctive situations (Martocchio, 2018).

Collective bargaining law may permit negotiations for employee paid leave benefits, although school districts generally may not establish a number of days below the state's legal requirement. Lost productivity, substitute costs, and benefit expenses contribute to an organization's overall paid leave expense (National Council on Teacher Quality, 2019).

According to the U.S. Department of Labor (2019c), 91% of primary and secondary schoolteachers across the nation have a fixed number of sick days per year in accordance with state law or the negotiated labor agreement. The U.S. Department of Labor (2019c) further indicated in the March 2019 reporting period that 2% of the teachers who participated in sick leave retain the opportunity to utilize as many sick leave days as needed. A consolidated leave provision bundles an arranged number of days for multiple purposes (i.e., illness, personal, and vacation). Nationally, 28% of elementary and secondary teachers participated in such an arrangement.

Military leave stands as an unpaid work interruption granted to employees who are active members of U.S. Reserves or a state's National Guard. The Uniformed Services Employment and Reemployment Rights Act of 1994 (USERRA) entitles an employee with unpaid leave up to five years, when called to active military duty during private or public employment (Martocchio, 2018).

With military service under USERRA, employees may continue their district's health insurance benefits up to 24 months. For active service lasting 90 days or less, the law stipulates that the staff member must return to the same position or a position the military employee would have attained if not called to duty. USERRA further sanctions seniority, salary increases, and other acquired benefits for returning employees (Martocchio, 2018).

Family Medical Leave Act of 1993 (FMLA) commands employers with 50 or more employees to grant unpaid leave for an employee's serious health condition; birth, adoption, or foster care of an employee's child; and a critical health condition of a spouse, son, daughter, or parent. Under FMLA, public and private employers must allow eligible employees up to 12 weeks of unpaid leave, job protection, and the continuation of health insurance benefits. School staff members, however, may choose to utilize paid sick leave in accordance with district policies instead of unpaid FMLA leave in these situations (Martocchio, 2018).

Group Medical Insurance

Group medical insurance designates a voluntarily offered fringe benefit that an employer grants to an employee and eligible family members under a district or state policy. This benefit subsidizes employee expenses related to provider care, hospitalization, surgery, medical equipment, and prescription drugs. Group health insurance, on the other hand, bundles coverages for medical, vision, and dental insurances. Employers in group medical or health plans usually shoulder the bulk of insurance costs, although employees frequently share expenses (Martocchio, 2018).

According to the U.S. Department of Labor (2019c), 95% of full-time primary and secondary school employees had access to group health insurance during the March 2019 reporting period, with 84% actually participating in a plan. Health and medical insurance offerings differ from school district to district and state to state, although selections usually include administrative structures, plan design types, eligibility status, benefit levels, and employee along with employer contribution shares.

To deliver healthcare benefits to eligible enrollees, school districts in 30 states (see table 2.1) must independently purchase a group medical insurance plan for employees. Twelve of those 30 states permit districts to participate in a consortium (C). Districts in 20 states and the District of Columbia may procure group medical insurance by participating in a plan sponsored by the state; however, employees may opt out of coverage. Texas school districts with less than 500 students must participate in the state plan, although employees are not obligated to accept the coverage (National Conference of State Legislatures, 2018).

A health benefit insurance consortium, chartered by the state or a private enterprise, denotes a group of school districts and/or governmental entities (i.e., townships, cities, and counties) that band together to procure group medical or health insurance and pool risks. The consortium administers various independent insurance plan(s), collects and holds each district's premiums in trust, disburses payments to providers, and processes claims, when a third-party administrator (TPA) is not employed (Martocchio, 2018).

Although specific benefit plans offered to employees may vary by states, districts, or consortiums, group health plans typically provide a full range of medical, hospital, and prescription drug coverage. Ancillary benefits may include dental and vision insurance (Martocchio, 2018). Table 2.1 presents collective bargaining law (i.e., negotiations) related to fringe benefits and district group medical or health insurance plan procurement methods by jurisdiction.

A plan sponsor denotes an employer (e.g., school district or state) or organization (e.g., consortium) that extends a group health or medical plan to its employees and eligible members. The health insurance premium represents either the employer's or employee's monthly health benefit payment (Martocchio, 2018).

Although premiums vary significantly across the country due to regional healthcare costs and local personnel decisions, the U.S. Department of Labor (2019c) nationally reported that primary and secondary school employers' premium share of the entire expense for health benefits averaged 83% for a

Table 2.1 Collective Bargaining Laws and District Health Insurance Procurement

Jurisdiction	*Bargaining Law*	*Independent Procurement*	*State Plan*	*Jurisdiction*	*Bargaining Law*	*Independent Procurement*	*State Plan*
Alabama	Not Allowed	X		Nebraska	Mandatory	X	
Alaska	Mandatory	X		Nevada	Mandatory	X	
Arizona	Not Allowed	X–C		New Hampshire	Not Addressed		
Arkansas	Permissive		X	New Jersey	Mandatory	X–C	X
California	Mandatory	X–C		New Mexico	Not Addressed		
Colorado	Permissive			New York	Mandatory	X–C	X
Connecticut	Permissive	X		North Carolina	Not Allowed		X
Delaware	Mandatory		X	North Dakota	Not Addressed	X	
Florida	Mandatory	X–C	X	Ohio	Permissive	X–C	
Georgia	Not Allowed		X	Oklahoma	Mandatory		X
Hawaii	Mandatory		X	Oregon	Mandatory		
Idaho	Mandatory	X		Pennsylvania	Permissive	X–C	
Illinois	Mandatory	X		Rhode Island	Not Addressed	X	
Indiana	Mandatory	X		South Carolina	Not Allowed		X
Iowa	Prohibited	X		South Dakota	Not Addressed	X	
Kansas	Mandatory	X		Tennessee	Mandatory	X–C	X
Kentucky	Not Addressed		X	Texas	Not Allowed	X–C	X (>500 staff)
Louisiana	Not Addressed		X	Utah	Not Addressed	X	X
Maine	Mandatory	X–C		Vermont	Prohibited		X
Maryland	Mandatory		X	Virginia	Not Allowed	X	X
Massachusetts	Not Addressed	X		Washington	Not Addressed		X
Michigan	Mandatory	X		Washington, DC	Mandatory		X
Minnesota	Mandatory	X–C		West Virginia	Permissive		X
Mississippi	Not Addressed		X	Wisconsin	Mandatory	X–C	
Missouri	Mandatory		X	Wyoming	Not Addressed		X
Montana	Mandatory	X–C					

Sources: National Conference of State Legislatures (2018) and National Council on Teacher Quality (2019).

single plan and 64% for family coverage during the March 2019 reporting period.

Nationwide, a school district's monthly premium for single coverage averaged $538.12 during the March 2019 reporting period, and an employee paid $154.12 per month on average. Countrywide, districts averaged $1,063.53 in a monthly premium per employee for family coverage during the March 2019 reporting period, and an employee's share, on average, was $620.83 per month for family coverage (U.S. Department of Labor, 2019c).

A school district's payroll department collects the employees' insurance payments through deductions and merges employees' subsidies for the district's sum into a restricted fiduciary trust fund account. To establish the premium, insurance carrier (i.e., insurance company or insurer) actuaries apply a set of rating variables to compute the school district's health insurance premium with an experience-rated methodology (Martocchio, 2018).

An experience-rated methodology calculates a district's premium by examining actual claims for eligible district enrollees or reviewing the claim history for a risk pool of covered participants in the district, consortium, or state. In a community-rated approach, insurer actuaries compute premiums based on a specific geographical location, with consideration of the average actual health care or projected costs for eligible insurance participants (Martocchio, 2018).

When managing a group medical insurance program, the plan sponsor personnel must decide the program's administrative structure by choosing either a self-insured or a fully insured arrangement. Fifteen states utilized a self-funded structure. Idaho, North Carolina, Texas, Virginia, Washington, and Wisconsin direct fully insured state programs (Martocchio, 2018; Milliman, Inc., 2017; National Conference of State Legislatures, 2018).

Districts in a traditional fully insured program contract with an insurance carrier and compensate the insurer in advance to cover the providers' projected claims, carrier's operating expenses, and administrative costs. The insurance carrier's designated employees process the district's claims. A fully insured plan ordinarily is more expensive than a self-insured plan. Although the annual premium remains set in advance for a fully insured plan, the insurance company typically establishes a rate that greatly exceeds anticipated claims and expenses. Employees in this type of plan usually possess few incentives to use lower-cost services (Martocchio, 2018).

Self-insurance refers to a risk management technique where a district or the state reserves a pool of money in the budget to satisfy unexpected losses. When claim expenses become payable in a self-insured plan, the state, district, or consortium insurance trust fund account generally offsets the insurance expenses. Self-insured states and school districts assume direct financial responsibility for all the expenses from covered members' claims (Martocchio, 2018).

When the collected premiums do not exceed the charges in self-insured plans, the outstanding insurance trust account balance remains in reserve for future health insurance claims. When the charges exceed the collected premiums, the debt carries to the next month. When the district or state does not pay premiums in advance to an independent insurer, they may retain the unused funds for cash flow expenses (Martocchio, 2018).

Single and family coverages are other important distinctions that apply to fully insured and self-insured plans. Single coverage extends benefits only to the covered employee. Family coverage offers benefits to the covered employee and qualified dependents (Martocchio, 2018).

The plan sponsor personnel in a self-insured program defines the plan benefits, unless negotiable under collective bargaining law. The district staff processes claims, unless otherwise determined. The variable monthly expenditures within a self-insured plan include the payments for participants' dollar-for-dollar insured claims. Fixed costs may involve administrative fees and a stop-loss insurance premium, when in effect (De Paoli et al., 2017; Martocchio, 2018).

By selecting a self-insured option, as opposed to a fully funded method, this arrangement usually decreases administrative costs, maintains expense transparency, and increases plan efficiency by paying claims when processed. Because the employer assumes full liability and risk for all claims, uncertain monthly expenses and the uncontrollable timing of claims are budgeting challenges with self-funding. The practice of self-funding insurance, however, increased in district plans across the country because this type of insurance organization may lower overall costs (Martocchio, 2018).

Plan sponsor employees in a self-funded program, in many instances, contract with a TPA who is neither the policyholder nor the insurer. Although the TPA does not assume any financial liability within the plan, this support organization exclusively administers the plan, disburses payments to providers from the district's account, credits the claim reserve when available, generates and shares utilization reports, negotiates provider fees, and processes claims in accordance with the insurance plan document (Martocchio, 2018).

The TPA reviews employee healthcare claims, invoices the plan sponsor for paid claims on behalf of members, negotiates rates with medical service providers, and estimates the amount of necessary monies to pay healthcare expenses (Martocchio, 2018).

The plan document (i.e., benefit summary) describes the plan sponsor and eligible employees' rights and responsibilities; medical care coverages, exclusions, and limitations; and procedures to access benefits (Martocchio, 2018).

In order to mitigate a district's risk in a self-insured plan, the plan sponsor often utilizes a stop-loss carrier that reimburses the district for medical and/or pharmacy claims exceeding a predetermined threshold. The legal authority from each state's Department of Insurance to regulate stop-loss insurance widely varies from state to state; some states do not impose any regulations on stop-loss insurance in self-funded programs, while other states regulate strict standards for stop-loss insurance (De Paoli et al., 2017).

After the U.S. congressional passage of the Patient Protection and Affordable Care Act (2010) eliminated annual healthcare benefit limits, nationwide interest in stop-loss coverage grew because the number of catastrophic (i.e., high dollar) claims rose dramatically. Stop-loss insurance coverage became essential because most self-insured plan sponsors managed at least one high-cost claim in a given year (De Paoli et al., 2017).

Most stop-loss policies include coverage for medical and prescription drug claims, although some policies only cover medical claims or prescription drugs. A proven negotiation process for stop-loss insurance is a critical step to secure competitive rates. As a best practice, negotiations should identify reasonable individual and aggregate coverage limits along with judicious prescription drug levels to reduce the district expense on catastrophic claims (Aegis Risk, 2019).

Plan sponsor personnel may choose to purchase stop-loss coverage from a stop-loss insurance carrier. Some insurance companies assume the full liability of catastrophic claims, while others purchase reinsurance that transfers a portion of its risk to another insurance company for claims above a particular level (De Paoli et al., 2017).

A stop-loss insurance policy describes two coverages—an individual stop-loss amount and an aggregate stop-loss sum. Individual stop-loss coverage protects the district, when a covered participant has a single catastrophic claim or a series of claims that reach a particular cost point. Aggregate stop-loss coverage guards the district against collective individual claims above a set threshold and/or cumulative claims that do not reach the individual stop-loss level, but the district's aggregate claims reach a distinct point (Aegis Risk, 2019).

For example, when a district has a $50,000 individual stop-loss limit, the district remains responsible for claims up to $50,000 on an individual basis. The stop-loss carrier insures and reimburses the district on claims after the individual surpasses the $50,000 claim threshold in a calendar year (see figure 2.1).

When a district has 50 covered employees and 10 employees exceed the individual stop-loss threshold with this stop-loss coverage, the district must pay up to $500,000 in claims for those 10 employees, and the stop-loss carrier is responsible for collective costs above the individual $50,000 stop-loss point.

When 40 of the district's employees incur claims averaging $15,000 each, the district becomes responsible for $600,000; however, with the other

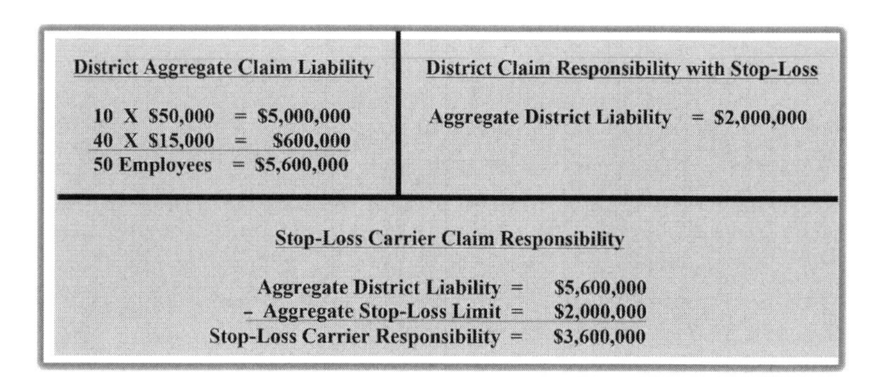

Figure 2.1 District and Stop-Loss Carrier Claim Responsibility

claims, the total liability surpasses the aggregate $2 million stop-loss coverage limit. Thus, the stop-loss carrier covers $3.6 million of the district's claims under the terms of this stop-loss policy. Figure 2.1 shows the district and stop-loss carrier claim responsibility for the above example.

De Paoli et al. (2017) stated that the cost of stop-loss insurance is not always immediately apparent because the cost of this type of policy often has four separate parts:

- stop-loss premium,
- plan sponsor's monthly claim fund contribution,
- TPA or insurance carrier fees and related costs, and
- advance funding repayment provision, when additional contributions to the fund become necessary to pay claims that exceed the fund balance.

Many stop-loss insurance policies indicate that premiums can increase at any time during the policy year, and even retroactively, when additional, unforeseen risks occur. District financial planning, therefore, remains problematic for stop-loss insurance. Some stop-loss insurance policies charge a provisional premium rate. The stop-loss carrier then adjusts the premium rate six months after the end of the policy period to reflect actual claims. Based on the provisions of the stop-loss insurance policy, a district's stop-loss insurance cost is quite expensive (De Paoli et al., 2017).

Actions to reduce your stop-loss premium and ensure adequate coverage include:

- analyzing the district's catastrophic claim history and medical trends yearly,

- requesting reductions with the current carrier when catastrophic claims decline,
- negotiating for stop-loss coverage, and
- employing an experienced broker or consultant (Aegis Risk, 2019).

Consortiums may also save a district money for health insurance in several ways. Because health insurance consortiums pool the resources of several school districts, they can leverage more powerful purchasing power to lower member (i.e., district) premiums. To rein in health insurance costs, a consortium's function may involve pooling risks; jointly negotiating insurance vendors, TPAs, and stop-loss insurance carriers; advising plan designs; and administering other tasks (Martocchio, 2018).

Pooling risks in a consortium allow the higher costs of less healthy individuals in the risk pool to offset the relatively lower costs of healthy people. Under state insurance law, a drawback to consortium participation is the maintenance of a mandated cash reserve. In order to fund unexpected losses sufficiently, reserve funds are necessary, but the consortium's assigned reserve amount may exceed an actuarially sound need (Martocchio, 2018).

Based on consortium regulations and state law, each consortium member may maintain ownership of its reserve balance and earn interest income on those reserves. Health benefit consortiums may operate a fully insured, self-insured, or hybrid self-insurance insurance structure. A fully insured health consortium contracts with an insurance company that collects premiums from members, pays healthcare claims, administers the plan, and assumes any financial risk should premiums not be sufficient to cover claims.

A self-insured health consortium, the most common type, collects and holds member premiums in a trust account and pays claims (Filla et al., 2016). With this type of consortium, the staff usually negotiates and purchases a stop-loss insurance policy with individual and aggregate coverages, when claims exceed determined thresholds.

In a hybrid self-insured plan, the consortium staff negotiates insurance plans, stop-loss insurance policies, and TPA agreements; contracts with a TPA to administer the district insurance plan; disperses funds for incurred claims; and holds districts accountable for their individual claim liability (Filla et al., 2016).

After considering the program format, plan sponsor decision makers may deliberate on the insurance delivery design—preferred provider organization (PPO), health maintenance organization (HMO), point of service (POS), exclusive provider organization (EPO), consumer-directed health plan (CDHP), or indemnity. State plans, as district plans, occasionally offer employees multiple delivery choices within the overall group health insurance plan. Unionized organizations may negotiate plan designs, when permitted by state collective bargaining law (Martocchio, 2018; Vines, Braceland, Rollins, & Miller, 2018).

Due to the increasing cost of health care, managed-care health plans (e.g., PPO, HMO, POS, and EPO) remain popular choices to reduce the plan sponsor and enrollee's medical insurance expenses. Plan sponsor personnel in a managed-care plan contract with healthcare providers and medical facilities to perform health services at an agreed-upon discounted fee. The managed-care plan structure encourages insured participants to receive medical care from a network of preapproved providers, even though enrollees may utilize services from providers outside the network at an extra cost (Martocchio, 2018; Vines et al., 2018).

With a wide latitude of design choices, Claxton, Rae, Long, Damico, and Whitmore (2019) reported that many firms across the country offered members only one plan type. Considering all choices, 49% of all plan sponsors nationwide granted medical insurance through a PPO, 29% offered consumer-directed plans, 16% supplied HMOs, 6% delivered POS, and less than 1% provided indemnity programs (Claxton et al., 2019). Because plan sponsors offered more than one delivery type, the sum of these percentages did not equal 100%.

Plan sponsor personnel in a PPO, the most popular managed-care design, contract with a group of healthcare providers within a network. In-network providers supply services at a discounted fee in exchange for the possibility of increased business. Participants may also receive health care from out-of-network providers without a major financial penalty (Martocchio, 2018; Vines et al., 2018).

In a PPO, however, the insured party does shoulder a higher share of the medical expense from an out-of-network provider than an in-network provider. Because PPOs are generally less restrictive than HMOs, participants have a greater choice of healthcare providers (Martocchio, 2018; Vines et al., 2018).

CDHPs have recently gained popularity after approval by federal and state legislations. CDHPs in a high-deductible health plan (HDHP) entrust enrollees to make decisions about their own health care, including financing a health savings account (HSA) or health reimbursement account (HRA). HDHPs encourage participants to utilize lower-cost providers because enrollees contribute a greater share of healthcare expense via a higher deductible than other plan types (Martocchio, 2018; Vines et al., 2018).

The HSA structure enables enrollees to set aside money up to the Internal Revenue Service pretax limit to pay for out-of-pocket expenses, including deductibles, copayments, coinsurance, prescription medications, vision expenses, and dental costs. An employer may elect to contribute financially to an employee's HSA; however, employees own their account and may add or withdraw dollars from the account at any time. Plan sponsor decision makers in some instances may permit an accumulation of monies in individual accounts over years (Vines et al., 2018).

The HMO, another type of managed-care plan, assigns a primary care physician who refers participants to in-network specialists and other healthcare professionals when necessary. When participants need medical services, they pay a nominal fee for in-network providers' services. When an enrollee receives services from an out-of-network provider in an HMO, the participant's out-of-pocket cost may be more expensive than in-network provider services, or the service may not be covered (Martocchio, 2018; Vines et al., 2018).

Although HMOs generally save money for participants and districts, covered members have a limited number of healthcare providers from which to obtain services than in a PPO. HMOs theoretically reduce district plan expenses by controlling specialist referrals and managing costs from in-network provider services (Martocchio, 2018; Vines et al., 2018).

A POS design, a PPO/HMO hybrid, is yet another managed-care plan design. Plan sponsor staff members in a POS contract with a number of healthcare providers in networks like a PPO or HMO. Eligible enrollees, however, choose between in-network or out-of-network providers at the point of service. This plan type becomes attractive to participants who want the benefits of a managed-care plan but do not want to be restricted by only receiving medical care from in-network providers (Martocchio, 2018; Vines et al., 2018).

In-network providers in a POS plan normally charge a discounted fee; out-of-network service providers generally invoice by the usual, customary, and reasonable (UCR) rate. The UCR rate designates the fees that healthcare providers typically charge for a given service in a geographical area. Out-of-network providers, therefore, do not assume the HMO fee structure restrictions based on a fixed, predetermined monthly payment regardless of provided care and the number of patients' visits (Vines et al., 2018).

In an EPO plan, an infrequently employed managed-care design, health or medical insurance participants may only use in-network primary care providers, hospitals, or specialists. When an eligible enrollee utilizes an out-of-network provider, the EPO plan does not cover any out-of-network expenses except for emergency care, urgent care outside of the service area, or critical medical services that lack an in-network provider (Martocchio, 2018).

Indemnity plans became increasingly expensive in the late 20th century; thus, this plan type decreased in popularity. Under an indemnity structure, commonly called a fee-for-service plan, an insured member is not required to choose a primary healthcare provider, hospital, or pharmacy (Martocchio, 2018; Vines et al., 2018).

The insured party in this design initially pays for health services and then submits a claim later to the insurance carrier for reimbursement. The enrollee usually pays an annual deductible (i.e., individual and/or family) before the insurer begins payments for covered medical services. At the time of patient service, the participant may pay a copayment, a fixed amount to share costs with the employer. Once having met the deductible, an indemnity plan typically pays claims at a set percentage of the UCR rate (Vines et al., 2018).

Most medical insurance plans subject members to deductibles, copayments, limitations, exclusions, and coinsurances regardless of the plan design. Coinsurance illustrates another form of cost sharing in a health or medical insurance plan when an insured person pays a percentage of expenses, after meeting the deductible amount.

An employee assistance program refers to the professional assessment, referral, and/or short-term counseling service offered to employees with alcohol, drug, domestic violence, or mental health problems that may affect job performance. The basic purpose of an employee assistance program is to promote an individual's well-being in a confidential and professional manner for the betterment of the work environment (Martocchio, 2018).

An employee assistance program decreases absenteeism, reduces employee accidents, lessens workers' compensation claims, improves employee retention, diminishes labor disputes, and reduces medical costs due to early identification and treatment of mental health along with substance abuse issues (Martocchio, 2018).

Outpatient prescription drug coverage often integrates with the covered members' medical insurance plan. Across the nation, 93% of teachers had access to outpatient prescription drug coverages during the March 2019 reporting period and 75% participated in a group health insurance policy or separate prescription drug policy (U.S. Department of Labor, 2019c).

Three kinds of prescription drug plans remain available to districts—medical reimbursement, prescription card, and mail-order prescription drug programs. These plans are usually associated with self-funded or independent indemnity plans. Similar to indemnity plans, medical reimbursement plans pay benefits after an employee meets an annual deductible. These plans offer coinsurance after the deductible, which is usually 80% of the prescription drug cost. The employee pays the difference. Maximum annual and lifetime benefit amounts vary based on the plan provisions (Martocchio, 2018).

A prescription card program functions like managed-care health plans by offering prepaid benefits with nominal copayments. Prescription card programs limit benefits to prescriptions filled at participating pharmacies, similar to managed-care arrangements for medical treatment. Copayment amounts vary from $5 to $50 per prescription. The amount depends upon whether the prescription meets or does not meet the plan criteria, such as the use of generic alternatives and formularies. Clinically appropriate formularies list cost-effective drugs. Participants pay lower copayments for formulary drugs (Martocchio, 2018).

A mail-order prescription drug program dispenses medications for chronic health conditions, such as high blood pressure or high cholesterol. Mail-order programs typically operate in combination with prescription card programs. The copay is generally much less for mail-order purchases than prescription card acquisitions; therefore, the staff should be encouraged to use mail-order services when appropriate (Martocchio, 2018).

Costs vary with prescription drug plans. Reimbursement plans normally remain the most expensive because pharmacies charge full retail price. This type of plan also encounters substantial administrative costs because an administrator evaluates each claim, applies deductibles, and prepares an explanation of benefits (Martocchio, 2018).

Prescription card and mail-order programs are usually less expensive than reimbursement plans because plan sponsors, TPAs, or insurance companies have negotiated lower prices in exchange for the possibility of higher prescription drug volume. Costs are additionally lower because participants pay copayments when they order prescriptions, and the pharmacy then bills the insurance company at a set interval (Martocchio, 2018).

Prescription drug plans often contain two other cost-containment features—formularies and multiple tiers. Formularies, therapeutically equivalent to more costly drugs, contain costs due to lower coinsurance or copayments. More restrictive plans limit coverage to a specified set of prescription drugs (Martocchio, 2018).

Multiple-tier prescription plans often specify three copayment levels for a prescription from the least to highest copayments—generic ($10 to $20 per prescription), formulary brand name ($25 to $40 per prescription), or nonformulary brand name ($40 to full price per prescription). Multiple-tier prescription plans steer employees to less expensive, equally effective prescription alternatives from more costly nonformulary medications. Multitier prescription plans may save plan sponsors considerable dollars, while still offering effective treatments based on less expensive alternatives (Martocchio, 2018).

Plan sponsor personnel face financial challenges in delivering quality employee health insurance, and decision makers often transfer rising costs onto the employee's premium, although changing any aspect of the health insurance benefit may prove difficult, when districts must negotiate plan modifications with union representatives. To effect change, school districts and states occasionally employ an appointed committee or task force to implement plan changes, examine expenditures, and recommend cost-containment strategies (Martinez, King, & Cauchi, 2016).

Educating the staff about the district's health insurance plan and cultivating buy-in among employees regarding the plan's vision, future alterations, and tactics to save expenses embody key strategies for the plan sponsor, an insurance committee, or task force to contain healthcare costs. When implementing changes, employees, however, may view shifting costs as compromising the health program's value (De Paoli et al., 2017).

The plan sponsor staff's intent should be to promote the best possible employee health outcomes and contain program costs instead of merely raising the employee's premium share or cutting benefits to reduce expenses. Plan sponsor personnel and/or task force members should scrutinize structures, plan designs, and healthcare providers along with prescription drug utilization patterns to find potential savings (Vines et al., 2018).

Although most districts and states already self-insure, this insurance structure affords an opportunity to save costs connected with actual insurance usage. Self-insured programs may also save plan sponsors between 5% and 6% in administrative costs alone in comparison to fully insured programs (De Paoli et al., 2017).

The enrollees in a self-insured program may become more responsible and responsive about their personal usage, which may lower employee and district expenses. Incorporating third-party administration and stop-loss insurance within the insurance structure may present savings too. Effective negotiations with TPAs and stop-loss carriers may also contain expenses (De Paoli et al., 2017).

When the plan sponsor staff contemplates a change in insurance carriers, they must address runoff claims with the existing carrier and be aware of lowball quotes by a new insurer. Runoff claims refer to follow-up claims incurred following policy termination related to claims encountered prior to the policy cancellation date. A termination provision in the existing insurance contract should stipulate that the insurer should remain liable and honor all associated claims after termination (De Paoli et al., 2017).

A lowball quote represents a persuasive sales technique in which an insurance sales representative offers services at an unusually low price and then markedly raises the premium after the first year. Talking to plan sponsors who recently enrolled with the new insurer may offer insight into annual price variations. Changing insurance companies, nevertheless, should be seamless with regard to exposure and coverages (De Paoli et al., 2017).

Because the health insurance premium correlates with overall utilization, enlarging the pool of insured participants may reduce expenses. As such, participating in a statewide or consortium risk pool affords potential cost saving, especially for small school districts. Combining small employer groups into a larger state or consortium pool may save money in the plan. By pooling the resources of several school districts or governmental entities, consortiums leverage greater purchasing power to obtain lower premiums and spread risk factors over a greater number of covered members (Riley et al., 2019).

Shifting to another plan design may result in lower district costs. Moving from an indemnity design into a PPO, POS, HMO, or EPO may reduce costs for the district and employee, although the latter plan designs may become more restrictive for participants. When considering a plan design change, the plan sponsor staff and/or task force members must anticipate the possibility of employee or union resistance due to changes in service options (De Paoli et al., 2017).

A gradual shift to steer participants toward another design instead of a dramatic conversion may ease resistance. Pinpointing the most effective balance of incentives and drawbacks to change long-term features remains critical. Lowering employees' copayments for preventive services may contain costs and increase participation (De Paoli et al., 2017).

A consumer-directed plan design is another option to offer employees that may contain costs, albeit a cost-sharing approach. HDHPs have the potential to control healthcare costs by providing employees' incentives to seek greater cost efficiency in their healthcare services (Martocchio, 2018).

By requiring enrollees to pay a greater share of the initial cost of care than other plans, HDHPs encourage employees to choose less expensive providers and may steer covered members toward better services. The process of searching for lower-cost providers denotes an underlying HDHP principle, which will likely raise employee awareness of healthcare services' expenses through comparisons of providers' assistances and prices (Martocchio, 2018).

Although enrollees in an HDHP plan may have a higher deductible than other plan designs, employees may experience lower personal monthly premiums than with other plans. The HDHP option with an incentive of a premium reduction, above all, may encourage employees to accept this plan type (Martocchio, 2018).

When decision makers and resulting health insurance plans support covered parties in making informed decisions for their personal care and providing financial incentives to promote healthy action, the district may reduce overall claim expenditures. A well-designed wellness program encourages opportunities for insured parties to address life choices that drive chronic disease charges (Martocchio, 2018).

A wellness program should encourage insured members to improve their general health conditions and detect diseases (e.g., high blood pressure, high cholesterol, or diabetes) at the onset. The program may offer enrollees free or lower-cost preventive care (e.g., smoking cessation, weight loss, stress management, and fitness club memberships), premium discounts, cash rewards, and/or inexpensive health screenings (Martocchio, 2018).

A wellness program, overall, normally improves employee health behaviors, reduces health risks, lessens healthcare costs, advances employee productivity, decreases staff absenteeism, improves employee recruitment and retention, builds and sustains positive employee morale, and saves the district and enrollees healthcare expenses (Martocchio, 2018).

Plan participants with chronic, long-term conditions who take a maintenance prescription drug should be educated and encouraged to use generic drugs along with an in-network mail prescription service. Because generic drugs are a reasonable alternative for the same care level as brand-name drugs, they offer potential to reduce health plan expenditures (De Paoli et al., 2017).

As an insurance plan provision to promote cost-effective outcomes and advocate for enrollees' health needs, TPA case management monitors services, approves care procedures and pharmaceutical needs, and holds healthcare providers accountable for supplying the most essential treatments and medications. This collaborative process between the healthcare provider, insurance carrier, and TPA facilitates, coordinates, and presents optimal care with plan savings (Martocchio, 2018).

Preauthorization and precertification, additional plan stipulations that accompany case management, refer to procedures when the TPA or insurance company preauthorizes a patient for coverage of a medical procedure or prescription drug. Health insurance companies or the TPA may require that patients meet certain criteria before authorizing coverage for particular treatments or prescriptions. Preauthorization and precertification typically do not apply in a medical emergency (Martocchio, 2018).

For preapproval, the TPA or insurance company generally requires that the patient's caregiver documents the patient's condition before prescribing treatment. When an enrollee does not obtain prior approval, the participant may be charged a penalty for noncompliance, although the insured's insurance card lists preauthorization and precertification for providers. In instances where the provider charges more than the UCR fee, the TPA staff will often question that expense (Martocchio, 2018).

Implementing tiered networks with incentives for participants to use specific networks may steer insured parties to the best providers and can contain costs. Tiered networks, similar to multitiered prescription drugs, may guide participants toward less expensive hospitals, physicians, and drugs and save plan costs, especially when less costly services afford an identical care level (Riley et al., 2019).

By pinpointing high-quality providers, particularly for elective procedures that drive a huge percentage of healthcare expenses, the plan sponsor staff can promote particular providers with participants. This strategy may save the district and enrollees' costs, without comprising patient care. Using reference pricing, which is the maximum price that a plan will pay for a specific procedure, plan decision makers can steer health insurance participants to less expensive services because the insured must pay the difference between the established reference rate and the overcharge (Riley et al., 2019).

With price referencing to determine provider costs, the plan sponsor should negotiate provider payment structures tied to Medicare's payment rates, which are known standards. In this payment arrangement, plan sponsors negotiate reimbursements at Medicare rates rather than network discounts. Basing reimbursement on Medicare rates offers several benefits—most providers accept the well-established Medicare payments and are adept at executing that payment system. The federal government additionally audits the Medicare payment system based on actual costs (Riley et al., 2019).

Telehealth (i.e., telemedicine), telebehavorial health, and capitation plans are other practices that can improve patient access and reduce expenses. Telehealth implies a system where patients receive healthcare services from providers in a remote location through a virtual connection with a registered nurse, therapist, or physician via a smartphone, tablet, and other electronic device; telebehavorial health signifies a subset of telemedicine that remotely connects patients with behavioral health providers. Telemedicine allows medical health professionals to provide patients with medical information and remotely monitor vital signs at a reduced rate (Center for Connected Health Policy, 2019).

Alaska and Mississippi are two state leaders in providing telehealth services with statewide programs that expand patient access to services and reduce insurance claim costs. Mississippi, for example, enacted a telehealth parity law that requires Medicaid, state employee health plans, and private insurers to provide coverage for telehealth services at the same level as in-person care. Telehealth programs have the potential to improve patient access, increase provider and system capacity, and promote the healthcare system (Center for Connected Health Policy, 2019).

According to Kansel (2019), an appointment via telemedicine costs average $79, compared to $146 for a doctor's office visit. Emergency room visits average $1,734 per occurrence.

Capitation (i.e., captives) plans, as an HMO approach, prepays a healthcare provider for services to a specific population, such as district insurance enrollees. With a capitation plan, healthcare providers must meet certain quality criteria by offering timely preventive screenings and promptly reviewing test results with patients. The providers in a capitated payment plan may receive bonuses, when patients stay healthy and avoid costly hospitalizations. This arrangement may deliver better patient outcomes, lower patient and district costs, and improve overall healthcare access than other approaches (Martocchio, 2018).

When plan sponsor personnel and insurance task force members endorse changing the insurance structure, modifications tend to have a better chance of employees' acceptance than without affirmation. Likewise, when plan sponsor personnel and insurance task force members conduct peer-to-peer outreach meetings with question and answer educational sessions led by early adopters, insurance participants tend to accept alterations better than without gatherings.

Unilaterally changing district plan designs without staff input is contentious because many public schools must negotiate plan modifications with union representatives and the staff. During such negotiations, bargaining union members are more apt to accept plan design adjustments, when fellow employee task force members endorse recommended alterations and evidence supports employee along with district savings instead of changing plans without proven verification of the advantages (De Paoli et al., 2017).

Other than insurance plan structure and design changes, collecting and analyzing data to understand a district's healthcare cost trends—both current and past—are critical. By employing data to effect change, plan sponsor personnel and/or task force members may better assess particular coverages than without the statistics. Data analytics refer to the process of inspecting, cleansing, transforming, interpreting, and modeling data, with the express purpose of discovering trends, patterns, and other information (De Paoli et al., 2017).

Analytic goals to improve participants' healthcare experiences, reduce insurance expenses, and support benefit plan decisions and changes serve both the insured member and the employer. Data analyses begin with detailed assessments of a plan's healthcare experiences, including historical claim and prescription drug utilization reviews, health risk assessments, and participations in the wellness program. Data analyses may reduce overall insurance costs and the ensuing employee and district premiums (De Paoli et al., 2017).

Predicting future employee health insurance utilization with trend data is helpful too. Predictive modeling depicts a statistical technique to forecast future behavior by analyzing historical and present health insurance data. Predictive modeling quantifies risk costs for individuals and groups of individuals enrolled in a health plan by identifying risk factors to target plan modifications, examining district and employee premium rates, categorizing insurance needs, comparing healthcare provider consumption, and shaping prospective directions (De Paoli et al., 2017).

For instance, when plan sponsor personnel and/or task force members predict that the district will have a number of catastrophic claims just beneath the individual and/or collective stop-loss limits, then decision makers should negotiate cost thresholds with stop-loss carriers to save the district money overall (De Paoli et al., 2017).

Plan sponsor staff and insurance committee members should employ data analytics and predictive modeling to identify plan savings through a utilization review. Group health plans must abide by applicable state and federal legislations. In conducting a utilization review and data analyses, reviewers must be cognizant of the Health Insurance Portability and Accountability

Act of 1996 (HIPAA) regulations that protect employees' health information privacy and security. HIPAA rules also mandate special enrollment period modifications and provide individuals with certain rights to their health information, particularly when a breach occurs (De Paoli et al., 2017; Martocchio, 2018).

To evaluate and control medical expenses, decision makers should conduct periodic assessments to detect indicators that drive a high percentage of costs and examine historical claim patterns that indicate service provider visits and categories, service frequency and charges, and members' care levels. To help the plan sponsor staff and/or task force members pinpoint cost drivers, the TPA should generate claim data (De Paoli et al., 2017).

When identifying insurance trend drivers, decision makers should specifically appraise the most noteworthy patterns, honor HIPAA regulations, and ask direct questions:

- Are there specific underutilized services within the plan?
- How frequently do participants avail themselves to in-network and/or out-of-network services?
- Is a subpopulation of covered lives disproportionately driving costs?
- Are there particular procedures or diseases disproportionately driving costs?
- Based on claims per employee, are the stop-loss insurance individual and aggregate thresholds too low, sufficient, or too high?
- What are the prescription drug trend utilizations and costs, including specialty drugs?
- Are there services not provided within a network (e.g., drugs and hospital service)?

Early detection of an enrollee's disease followed by less costly, invasive treatment is another analytic strategy to cut costs and improve care. When decision makers discover that the number of participants with diabetes increased 10% from the previous year, a rise in medical claims for diabetes treatments and related pharmaceutical needs will be forthcoming. Because diabetes is a disease related to weight, the plan sponsor should encourage and arrange a weight-loss program, which may reduce the number of claims, ease medication usage, and potentially arrest the disease's progression (De Paoli et al., 2017).

With pharmaceutical utilization, decision makers, for instance, may notice a plan's overall increase in drug claims above 10% from the previous year's claims due to higher prescription drug costs. The task force may further discover that general prescription drug utilization did not increase, but specialty drug expenses increased substantially, which may warrant a plan change.

For another cost-saving example, the plan sponsor decision makers, covered members, and TPA officials may wage a campaign to enroll a local hospital or provider into a network, when a majority of participants already utilize the facility or provider's services. This tactic may persuade the hospital administration or provider to join a network and offer discounted rates (De Paoli et al., 2017).

The Consolidated Omnibus Budget Reconciliation Act of 1985 (COBRA), a mandatory federal program, grants employees and eligible dependents a temporary continuation of group medical coverage, when an employee separates from employment due to a termination or reduction in force. Under COBRA, individuals who elect continued coverage must pay the full premium (i.e., district and employee's share). The district may also assess a 2% administrative fee. Although an employee utilizing COBRA bears all health insurance costs, a plan sponsor's experience rating may affect future district premiums (Martocchio, 2018).

The Patient Protection and Affordable Care Act (2010) mandates that public employers with at least 50 employees (e.g., certified and classified staff) provide health insurance to all employees who work an average of 30 or more hours per week. Given the relatively high cost of complying with the mandate and the financial penalties for noncompliance, employers may circumvent this order by cutting part-time staff or reducing staff hours (Martocchio, 2018).

Eliminating many annual and lifetime benefit limitations, allowing young dependents under 26 years of age to remain on a parent's health insurance program, and requiring preventive services without expense to the employee represent other costly Patient Protection and Affordable Care Act stipulations (Martocchio, 2018).

The Trump administration modified a few of the Patient Protection and Affordable Care Act provisions via an executive order. These modifications, however, did not affect school districts (Goldstein, 2018). Because health care and medical insurance remain such hot topics, school administrators and aspiring administrators should remain vigilant in keeping abreast of current and future developments. Future unfunded laws related to health care may raise group health or medical insurance costs and propose few alternatives to offset increased expenses.

Group Dental Insurance

Dental insurance insures a portion of the costs associated with preventive care and treatment of dental conditions. The plan sponsor staff may purchase and grant dental benefits with enrollment in a group health insurance plan or separate policy. Dental insurance resembles medical insurance in many regards, although dental expenses stay much lower in cost and easier on the district budget than medical insurance. Dental treatment generally emphasizes prevention, as opposed to medical insurance, which often applies to an illness, injury, or disease (Martocchio, 2018).

The U.S. Department of Labor (2019c) reported that 57% of full-time elementary and secondary school employees across the country had access to group dental insurance during the March 2019 reporting period. About 77% actually participated in a plan when available.

Dental benefit plans have three basic design structures—service corporation, maintenance organization (HMO), and indemnity plans. Service corporation plans remain the prevailing design, accounting for 74% of all plans across the country. The least offered plan is the indemnity arrangement (Martocchio, 2018).

Service corporations are state-owned and state-administered dental association nonprofit organizations. Participants in a service corporation type of plan may receive benefits for covered services from an in-network or out-of-network dental care provider. Service corporation plans, however, penalize enrollees by granting a smaller benefit for using an out-of-network provider instead of an in-network provider (Martocchio, 2018).

Enrollees in a dental HMO receive services from a primary dental care provider. The in-network dental care provider may refer the insured party for services outside the network. A capitation plan is common among dental HMOs where the plan sponsor prepays an in-network dental care provider a guaranteed payment each month. The capitated provider then offers contracted services at a reduced cost to enrollees (Martocchio, 2018).

The insured under an indemnity dental plan generally may choose any dental care provider for services and receives reimbursement for a portion of the costs. In an indemnity dental plan, service providers often set UCR fees. The insurance company reimburses claims based on the performed procedures and provisions in the benefit plan (Martocchio, 2018).

Similar to group medical insurance, the plan sponsor may finance dental insurance via self-insured or fully insured plans. The plan sponsor decision makers in a self-insured plan choose the plan-of-benefits, deductibles, copayments, coinsurances, and annual benefit maximum limits, unless state collective bargaining law applies. The plan sponsor pays enrollee claims from a trust account with the district and employees' premiums. A TPA may process claims for plan sponsor officials (Anthem Blue Cross and Blue Shield, 2019).

A fully insured plan typically represents a business arrangement between a plan sponsor and dental insurance company. The plan sponsor in a fully insured plan contributes a fixed monthly premium to a dental insurance carrier based on the benefit plan. The insurance carrier assumes all of the risks associated with enrollee claims and accordingly sets the premium (Anthem Blue Cross and Blue Shield, 2019).

Although levels of coverage may vary from plan to plan, South Carolina Public Benefits Authority (2018) reported that their dental insurance plans offered coverages for the following services—routine preventive and diagnostic care (e.g., oral examinations, cleanings and X-rays, fluoride treatments, and sealants) and nonroutine care (e.g., fillings, periodontal treatments, extractions, oral surgery, bridges, crowns, and orthodontics). The dental plan did not cover cosmetic procedures.

With a separate policy for dental insurance, plan sponsor officials may negotiate price quotations to compare premiums before enlisting with a carrier. Similar to medical insurance, the plan sponsor staff and/or task force members should utilize data analytics to discover trends and predictive modeling to forecast patterns in support of dental plan decisions and modifications to contain dental plan costs.

Group Vision Insurance

Vision insurance underwrites costs associated with eye care and eyewear. Similar to dental insurance, the plan sponsor staff may purchase and grant vision benefits with enrollment in a group health insurance plan or a separate policy. According to the U.S. Department of Labor (2019c), 34% of full-time elementary and secondary school employees across the country had access to vision insurance during the March 2019 reporting period, and 82% actually participated in a plan.

Many employers offer vision insurance as a cafeteria plan (i.e., benefit plan menu) where the employer gives employees several plan options, such as an HMO or PPO. HMOs remain the most restrictive plans for exams, with specified lenses/frames as the most common option. When an eye care provider in an HMO delivers a covered member lenses/frames outside the allowance, then the enrollee bears the extra cost (Martocchio, 2018).

PPOs, on the other hand, steer employees to a network of participating eye care providers who have agreed to provide services for a negotiated rate. The insurance carriers or plan decision makers solicit providers to participate in a network with the provider anticipating increased patient volume. The provider, in return, agrees to discounted costs. When using an in-network provider, employees in this type of plan usually have a number of benefits insured at 100% of the expense or pay a minimal copayment (Martocchio, 2018).

When an insured enrollee visits an out-of-network provider, the participant's out-of-pocket expense is typically greater with UCR charges than the cost within a network. Many vision plans, following the patterns seen in medical plans, permit pretax dollars automatically deducted by the employer in the form of flexible spending accounts, HSAs, or HRAs (Martocchio, 2018).

A vision plan often restricts the enrollee's number of eye care provider visits (e.g., 12 or 24 months) in a year or utilize a covered category. The schedule of benefits is easy for employees to understand because the plan normally states usage frequency and monetary caps, which are maximum allowances related to eye health and maintenance, such as routine eye examinations and testing, corrective eyewear (e.g., particular lenses/frames discounts), and eye surgery (Martocchio, 2018).

When permitted by state collective bargaining law, school boards may be obligated to bargain with union representatives on the schedule of benefits, service limitations, and other plan provisions. Contact lenses and Lasik surgery, considered cosmetic extras, are not generally included as a covered benefit, unless prescribed for medical reasons (Martocchio, 2018).

The risk pool group's rating sets the plan sponsor's vision premium, similar to other insurances. To set the annual vision premium, insurance carrier actuaries examine and factor the school district's plan design, preferred provider networks, claim history, number of covered members, group characteristics, fee trends, administrative costs, and geographical location. The vision plan services, benefit limits, and permitted number of annual visits covered by the plan generally drive the premium rate (Martocchio, 2018).

By understanding the pricing variables that affect cost, plan sponsor officials may request price quotations to compare premiums.

Group Life and Disability Insurance

Life and disability insurances are other common employee benefits in the United States. According to the U.S. Department of Labor (2019c), 83% of primary and secondary employees had access to life insurance benefits during the March 2019 reporting period, and 98% actually participated in life insurance benefits.

Upon employment and until job separation, employees may be automatically enrolled in a group term life insurance plan. A life insurance policy affords an employee's survivor(s) a death benefit. The named policy beneficiary, usually a spouse and/or child(ren), receives the allowance. The typical employee death benefit is either a set dollar amount or a sum based on a multiple factor (e.g., 1.5) of an employee's gross salary (Martocchio, 2018).

School districts, subject to negotiations in unionized settings, usually pay the full premium for employee life insurance; however, employees may share the expense. An insurance company administers the plan with the premium based on a prospective or retrospective experience rating. To set the premium, life insurance actuaries evaluate the insurance carrier's risk by examining the number of insured employees, cash limits, employees' ages, and benefit stipulations.

A summary plan with all the policy conditions contains the coverage levels, plan features, and exclusions. A group term life insurance policy, in difference to a whole life policy, usually does not include a cash or surrender-value provision (Martocchio, 2018).

In addition to group term life insurance, employers normally deliver an accidental death and dismemberment (AD&D) insurance, as an endorsement (i.e., rider) on the life insurance policy. When the employee's death is the result of an accident, this circumstance usually reimburses the survivor(s) a lump-sum amount or a multiple (e.g., 2.5) of the employee's gross salary (Martocchio, 2018).

When a body dismemberment occurs, this endorsement offers financial assistance during recovery and rehabilitation. Although dismemberment percentages differ according to the plan, the most common payment structure is 50% of the death benefit per limb and 100% for the loss of multiple limbs (Martocchio, 2018).

Short- and long-term disability insurances are two other possible endorsements within a life insurance policy. To qualify for a short-term disability due to an illness or accident unrelated to the job, the employee must generally remain off work for five to six days. Short-term disability insurance often replaces income on a percentage of net salary up to 26 weeks (Martocchio, 2018).

When an employee is unable to return to full-time work beyond the short-term disability time frame, long-term disability insurance covers the situation, with ordinary income replacement percentages ranging from 50% to 80% of an employee's gross salary. This benefit continues until the individual returns to suitable work based on education, training, or experience; attains normal retirement age; or dies (Martocchio, 2018).

According to the U.S. Department of Labor (2019c), 22% of primary and secondary school systems offered short-term disability insurance for the March 2019 reporting period, and 40% of districts provided long-term disability insurance. When an employee needs short-term disability coverage, 96% of the covered teachers utilized this benefit during the March 2019 reporting period, and 96% used long-term disability as needed. Short- and long-term disability insurances were only 0.2% of public employees' full compensation during the March 2019 reporting period (U.S. Department of Labor, 2019b).

School districts may self-insure or fully insure a disability income benefit plan. While employers face less risk in self-insuring short-term disability, long-term disability may be catastrophic; therefore, a fully insured plan with an insurance company covering the risk remains the best course for districts (Martocchio, 2018).

Although competitive bid law in most states does not obligate school districts to bid or acquire quotes for insurances (i.e., life, AD&D, and short- and long-term disabilities), a district may elect to request price quotations to compare costs. Like other types of insurance, a cost analysis, particularly for long-term disability with clear provisions on return-to-work language, case management, and behavioral health circumstances, may lower the expense (Martocchio, 2018).

Pension Assurance

With pension laws during the 19th century across the country, public and private sector employers could amend or eliminate employee retirement benefits at any time. Most full-time professional workers today expect and demand some kind of pension assurance, and pension expectations for employees in the education field remain the same as other professions. Legal authorizations protect state employees' past and/or future retirement benefits in various ways—state constitution, contractual or statutory language, or property rights' provisions (The Pew Charitable Trusts, 2019b). Because state employees' pension plans persist in flux, school personnel must remain aware of proposed and adopted changes in their state's retirement system, particularly for personal reasons.

Most states maintain separate retirement systems for public servants (e.g., classified and certified school employees, police officers, firefighters, and politicians). Most states pool and hold public pension assets in distinct fiduciary trust accounts and generally invest retirement funds in diversified investment portfolios. District employees and school systems, similar to other organizations, prefund retirement payments (Brainard & Brown, 2018).

According to the U.S. Department of Labor (2019c), 95% of full-time elementary and secondary school employees in the United States had access to state pension benefits during the March 2019 reporting period. Upon retirement, 85% of full-time primary and secondary school employees in the United States participated in state pension plans.

Each state regulates the retirement plan's primary benefit options—defined benefit (DB), defined contribution (DC), cash balance (CB), or a hybrid (H) program. States may offer a variety of pension plan choices to retirees, and participation varies from mandatory membership in a DB plan or DC plan to voluntary participation. The DB plan remains the dominate retirement configuration across the nation (Aldeman & Rotherham, 2019). Thirty-three states (see table 2.2) mandated a DB pension plan.

About 88% of public schoolteachers had access to DB pension plans in the United States during the March 2019 reporting period. Nationally, school districts, on average, contributed 17% of each teacher's salary toward pensions. States fund this assurance through a combination of employer subsidies, active employee contributions, and pension investment earnings (Aldeman & Rotherham, 2019; U.S. Department of Labor, 2019c).

A DB pension plan normally grants an employee with a specific monthly income at retirement after becoming vested (i.e., right to the benefit based on a predetermined employment length and age). Vested employees collect their particular payment based on a formula that factors the member's final average salary (FAS), retirement age, years of service, and designated FAS percentage into the equation (Aldeman & Rotherham, 2019).

The U.S. Department of Labor (2019c) indicated that 35% of primary and secondary public educators across the country had access to a DC retirement plan during the March 2019 reporting period, and 13% actually participated in this plan type. The employee and employer in this pension plan type contribute a percentage of the worker's salary into the state pension fund. The employee does not obtain a fixed monthly income upon retirement eligibility, as opposed to the DB plan. Based on the employer and/or employee's contributions plus investment earnings, the employee may collect the balance or a portion of the balance upon retirement in his or her account (Martocchio, 2018).

Defined contribution plans supply each employee a range of investment options that the pension member individually manages. The employee, therefore, assumes all the investment risk, while the employer typically fulfills their obligation with a specified contribution. Alaska and the District of Columbia offer school employees a mandatory DC program; Florida, Ohio, and South Carolina present a DC plan as an optional program (Brainard & Brown, 2018).

A number of hybrid retirement plans have evolved in the public sector. Hybrid plans differ according to contributions, enrollment, and investment choices. Hybrid plans with a mandatory or optional DB and/or DC plan provision maintain twofold coverages by combining key elements from each type. In a hybrid plan, the employee individually manages his or her personal investment account and collects a coordinated pension through a lifetime annuity. Eight states (Arizona, Connecticut, Michigan, Pennsylvania, Rhode Island, Tennessee, Utah, and Virginia) offer hybrid plans (Brainard & Brown, 2018).

Cash balance retirement plans grant employees an annuity or a lump-sum (i.e., accumulated cash balance) payment upon retirement based on the employee and employer's contributions, guaranteed interest rate on contributions, and additional investment dividends in excess of the guarantee when warranted. Members in this plan type may not choose the manner in which the state invests the retirement funds. Two states (Kansas and Kentucky) offer CB plans for newly hired state or educational employees or both (Brainard & Brown, 2018; Martocchio, 2018). Table 2.2 lists each jurisdiction's primary pension type.

Since the 2008 economic market crash, many states lost assets in their state retirement fund; however, curtailing pension income has not been successfully legislated by any state at this time. Because of the 2008 recession, many states, however, instituted a number of adjustments to their public sector retirement programs to reduce the state's investment risks and avoid future unfunded liabilities (Brainard & Brown, 2018).

Pension reforms include raising employee's vesting age and/or service year requirements, reducing or eliminating cost-of-living adjustments, or steering employees into the Patient Protection and Affordable Care Act market exchange. Vesting refers to an employee's nonforfeitable rights to pension benefits (Martocchio, 2018).

Table 2.2 Primary Pension Type(s)

Jurisdiction	*Pension Type(s)*	*Jurisdiction*	*Pension Type(s)*
Alabama	Mandatory DB	Nebraska	Mandatory CB within a DB
Alaska	Mandatory DC	Nevada	Mandatory DB
Arizona	Mandatory DB	New Hampshire	Mandatory DB
Arkansas	Mandatory DB	New Jersey	Mandatory DB
California	Mandatory DB	New Mexico	Mandatory DB
Colorado	Mandatory DB	New York	Mandatory DB
Connecticut	Mandatory DB	North Carolina	Mandatory DB
Delaware	Mandatory DB	North Dakota	Mandatory DB
Florida	Choice of DB or DC	Ohio	Choice of DB, DC, or H
Georgia	H with a choice DB or DC	Oklahoma	Mandatory DB
Hawaii	Choice of DB or H	Oregon	Mandatory H
Idaho	Mandatory DB	Pennsylvania	Mandatory DB
Illinois	Mandatory DB	Rhode Island	Mandatory H
Indiana	Pension Gratuity Choice	South Carolina	Choice of DB or DC
Iowa	Mandatory DB	South Dakota	Mandatory DB
Kansas	Mandatory CB within a DB	South Dakota	Mandatory DB
Kentucky	Mandatory CB within a DB	Tennessee	Mandatory H
Louisiana	Mandatory DB	Texas	Mandatory DB
Maine	Mandatory DB	Utah	Choice of DC or H
Maryland	Mandatory DB	Vermont	Mandatory DB
Massachusetts	Mandatory DB	Virginia	H (DB with Mandatory DC)
Michigan	H (DB with DC Optional)	Washington	Choice of DB or H
Minnesota	Mandatory DB	Washington, DC	Mandatory DC
Mississippi	Mandatory DB	West Virginia	Mandatory DB
Missouri	Mandatory DB	Wisconsin	Mandatory DB
Montana	Mandatory DB		

Sources: Aldeman and Rotherham (2019) and Brainard and Brown (2018).

Unlike pension income benefits, most state laws do not legally protect postemployment healthcare coverage, although states commonly continue to offer retiree health insurance coverage. Many states adjusted benefits after the 2008 recession to rein in future obligations and take advantage of opportunities to save expenses afforded by legislation, such as the Patient Protection and Affordable Care Act (The Pew Charitable Trusts, 2019a).

Courts across the country have upheld the state's authority to cut retiree healthcare benefits. Courts also supported increasing retiree health insurance premiums, deductibles, and copayments; promoting wellness programs; changing health insurance plans to high-deductible designs with HSAs; and steering retirees into the Patient Protection and Affordable Care Act market exchange and Medicare advantage prescription drug plan (The Pew Charitable Trusts, 2019b).

As a component of the retirement program, 49 states and the District of Columbia impart medical insurance to vested retirees and individuals who attain the Medicare requirement age (i.e., 65 years) in accordance with the Social Security Amendments of 1965. Nebraska remains the only state that does not grant medical insurance to vested retirees, although Idaho does not offer newly hired public workers retirement healthcare coverage (Brainard & Brown, 2018; The Pew Charitable Trusts, 2016).

According to Brainard & Brown (2018) and The Pew Charitable Trusts (2016), medical insurance pension options in states include retirees who

- receive no subsidy toward medical insurance premiums,
- may purchase healthcare coverage through the state's medical insurance program,
- obtain a fixed subsidy toward Medicare medical insurance premiums,
- collect a specified healthcare coverage without an exact subsidy toward a medical insurance premium, and
- accept a medical insurance premium subsidy tied to the actual health insurance premium.

Vested retirees in Maine and New Hampshire collect up to 100% of the state's medical insurance premium (The Pew Charitable Trusts, 2016).

Alongside the conventional retirement plan, many states and school districts allow employees to contribute additional earnings during employment into a federally sanctioned, tax-sheltered 403(b) and/or a 457(b) deferred compensation plan (Brainard & Brown, 2018).

The tax-sheltered 403(b) retirement savings program defines a voluntary payroll deduction approach where employees may set aside a portion of their compensation and self-select investments. When the employee separates from said employer prior to age 59½, the employee may not accept distributions in a 403(b) program without a tax penalty (Martocchio, 2018).

Employees in a 457(b) program, similar to 403(b) plans, contribute tax-sheltered dollars into a retirement savings account. A 457(b) plan offers a menu of permissible investment options similar to a 403(b) plan. In contrast with 403(b) plans, when the employee separates from said employer in a 457(b) plan, the employee may accept distributions at any age without penalty. When continuing to work for the employer that sponsored a 457(b) plan, the worker cannot accept any distributions until the age of 70½ years without a penalty. The employee in 403(b) and 457(b) plans pays income tax upon payment distributions (Martocchio, 2018).

Social Security is another retirement option for many educators. The Social Security Act (1935) excludes federal, state, and local government employees from mandatory coverage, unless the state legislature has passed a law to include Social Security as a retirement benefit. When states had the opportunity to extend Social Security to public sector employees in the 1950s, 30 states (see table 2.3) chose to authorize coverage with payroll deductions. When the state retirement system allows Social Security deductions, employers contribute 6.2% of the employee's salary and employees contribute 1.45% (Martocchio, 2018; Schmitz & Aldeman, 2017).

Eleven states and the District of Columbia in the 1950s chose not to allow Social Security withdrawals for public employees during employment. In nine states, coverage varies because state law defers the decision to withdraw Social Security deductions to individual school districts. Legislators in the states that disallowed Social Security withdrawals believed that retirees would receive better retirement coverage through state pension plans alone instead of a combination of benefits from the state retirement plan and Social Security (Aldeman & Rotherham, 2019; Schmitz & Aldeman, 2017).

When employees in the states and District of Columbia that do not permit Social Security payroll deductions during employment have earned the necessary quarters working in the private sector and reached eligible retirement age, they may qualify for Social Security benefits at a reduced rate (Aldeman & Rotherham, 2019; Schmitz & Aldeman, 2017). Table 2.3 shows Social Security benefits afforded to school personnel by jurisdiction.

For significant reforms to state retirement systems by state (Brainard & Brown, 2018), see https://www.nasra.org/files/Spotlight/Significant%20 Reforms.pdf.

Table 2.3 Social Security Benefits

Jurisdiction	*Varies*	*None*	*Authorized Deductions*	*Jurisdiction*	*Varies*	*None*	*Authorized Deductions*
Alabama			X	Nebraska			X
Alaska		X		Nevada		X	
Arizona			X	New Hampshire			X
Arkansas			X	New Jersey			X
California		X		New Mexico			X
Colorado		X		New York			X
Connecticut		X		North Carolina			X
Delaware			X	North Dakota	X		
Florida			X	Ohio		X	
Georgia	X			Oklahoma	X		
Hawaii			X	Oregon			X
Idaho			X	Pennsylvania			X
Illinois		X		Rhode Island	X		
Indiana			X	South Carolina			X
Iowa			X	South Dakota			X
Kansas			X	Tennessee			X
Kentucky		X		Texas		X	
Louisiana		X		Utah			X
Maine	X			Vermont			X
Maryland		X		Virginia			X
Massachusetts			X	Washington			X
Michigan			X	Washington, DC		X	
Minnesota	X			West Virginia			X
Mississippi			X	Wisconsin	X		
Missouri	X			Wyoming			X
Montana	X			Total	9	12	30

Sources: Aldeman and Rotherham (2019) and Schmitz and Aldeman (2017).

Professional Liability Insurance

School personnel in America's schools work in a high-risk environment, and every day staff members face the possibility of a lawsuit against them. Teachers and administrators resolve more than a thousand decisions a day with the vast majority involving student interactions. Teachers and administrators occasionally react to situations with little time to contemplate long-term implications of actions or reactions.

School employees become particularly vulnerable to lawsuits concerning tort liability issues, which implicate accountable actions that allegedly cause physical injury and/or emotional damage to another person. When school employees breach their duty of care, they become liable for damages or injuries. Staff members predominantly maintain a responsibility for their students' safety and welfare by averting neglectful and wanton acts. Accidents, however, occur in schools under the best circumstances (Alexander & Alexander, 2019).

Although school systems procure general liability insurance for district protection against personal injury or damages on school property, districts also remain responsible for personal claims against employees that result from a civil wrong (i.e., tort), negligent acts, bodily injury, or defamation. Although state immunity statutes protect school systems from employee misbehavior, courts do permit lawsuits against districts and individuals regardless of immunity. Districts, in general, must defend and indemnify (i.e., hold harmless) employees against individual liability (Alexander & Alexander, 2019).

To protect the district as well as employees, many states legally mandate that school districts supply staff members with professional liability insurance, which may be an endorsement on the district's general liability insurance policy or in a separate policy. Exposures include failing to supervise a classroom properly; faults in responding to, reporting, or preventing asserted bullying; and lapses in informing proper authorities in suspected child abuse situations. Employment liability lawsuits may entail allegations of sexual harassment, wrongful termination, and discrimination (Alexander & Alexander, 2019).

A professional liability insurance policy exhibits two kinds of limits: per occurrence, which denotes the maximum amount the insurer will reimburse for any one claim during the policy's life, and aggregate, which designates the maximum amount the insurer will compensate in total claims for the policy's lifetime (Alliant Insurance Services, 2019).

Policies express limitations by occurrence/aggregate; therefore, a $1 million/$3 million policy insures up to $1 million for any one claim during the policy period and up to $3 million for all claims during the policy's lifetime. Because these policy limits establish the amount of school and employee coverage, policy limits have a huge impact on the cost of professional liability insurance (Alliant Insurance Services, 2019).

Unemployment Insurance

Unemployment insurance furnishes temporary income assistance to individuals who become unemployed without any fault of their own until reemployed. Guided by the federal Unemployment Tax Act (1939) and state laws, legislation obligates employers to institute employee unemployment insurance; therefore, a school employee, certified or classified, may be eligible for unemployment compensation benefits, when the staff member does not have a contract for the upcoming academic cycle, or the district does not provide reasonable assurance of imminent employment (Martocchio, 2018).

Although states have a great deal of autonomy in establishing and operating their unemployment insurance program, the U.S. Department of Labor oversees each state's system. The U.S. Department of Labor (2019a) qualified that employers in 47 states and the District of Columbia hold unemployment trust fund accounts for unemployment insurance on behalf of their employees; however, employees in Alaska, New Jersey, and Pennsylvania contribute a minimal unemployment withholding tax. School systems in these three states withhold the charge by a percentage of an employee's gross wages (e.g., Alaska, 0.5% to 1.0%; New Jersey, 0.3825%; and Pennsylvania, 0.08%).

Employer unemployment insurance premiums vary by percentages of the organization's aggregate payroll salary. States maintain two means to finance unemployment claims, and employers may subsidize unemployment insurance by a prefunded state unemployment insurance premium or a direct benefit reimbursement. In a prefunded unemployment insurance system, a district joins other private and public state employers (U.S. Department of Labor, 2019a).

To establish a district's annual unemployment insurance premium, states employ an experience-rated method with a direct relationship to the district's unemployment risk based on objective factors, such as the number of previous employee claims and the size of the employer's workforce. The state department of unemployment staff distributes monies when necessary. Because a district realizes the annual premium in advance, the CFO/treasurer may accordingly budget the cost, which is simple in a prefunded system (Martocchio, 2018).

When unemployment claims exceed the premium, the state unemployment insurance system honors the claims, but the district can expect a premium increase in subsequent years. Because school districts typically maintain low unemployment rates, they may pay a higher premium in a prefunded system than a reimbursement program. In a prefunded system, states support all employers' needs in the state pool (U.S. Department of Labor, 2019a).

The benefit reimbursement option, permitted by Section 3309 of the Federal Unemployment Tax Act, allows nonprofit employers (i.e., school districts) to opt out of the prefunded system and only reimburse the state for actual unemployment claims. Utilizing the benefit reimbursement option, school districts avoid socialized costs of prefunded state programs (U.S. Department of Labor, 2019a).

A stable reimbursement method to compensate employees generally guarantees fewer claims and lower benefit charges; however, this option does not provide protection against excessive unemployment claims due to unprotected liabilities. With this method the district business office staff submits quarterly payments into the state's unemployment trust fund for direct applicant claims (U.S. Department of Labor, 2019a).

Unemployment compensation insurance costs may be contained, when school officials understand their state unemployment compensation law and practice sound personnel procedures, including properly documenting employee discharges. To decide between a prefunded or a benefit reimbursement system, school personnel should examine the propensity for district unemployment and monitor the trust reserve balance. Claim management firms will assist school systems in performing an unemployment savings analysis to control unemployment insurance costs and deciding the best method to finance unemployment claims (Lucki, 2017).

Workers' Compensation Insurance

The first comprehensive workers' compensation insurance program in the United States, enacted federally in 1908, protected only federal civilian workers. Every state adopted similar workers' compensation legislation for all employees thereafter. By state law, private and public employers must provide a range of assistance (e.g., medical care, case management, cash benefit for lost work, partial or permanent disability income, and vocational rehabilitation services) to employees who are injured or contract an illness while on the job. When an employee dies in a work-related incident, the beneficiary receives a cash settlement through the workers' compensation program (Martocchio, 2018).

This managed-care system strikes a balance between employers and employees. Employees collect benefits regardless of the party at fault for the incident, and employers get protection from lawsuits by injured employees who may seek monetary damages for pain and suffering (McLaren, Baldwin, & Boden, 2018; Szymendera, 2017).

Workers' compensation insurance, in various forms, served in excess of 90% of all employees in the United States during the March 2019 reporting period. Employers in 47 states fully finance this no-fault insurance; however, workers in Washington, Oregon, and New Mexico contribute a part of the workers' compensation insurance cost through payroll deductions or charges. Every state except Texas and the District of Columbia mandates that public, nonpublic, and charter school districts provide workers' compensation insurance to employees (McLaren et al., 2018).

Each state maintains a workers' compensation agency with core responsibilities to inform stakeholders of their roles, rights, and responsibilities; process claims; facilitate dispute resolutions; and track worker outcomes. Because state law governs workers' compensation insurance, each state's system differs in program details, but the general structure, obligations, and procedural rules remain the same from state to state (McLaren et al., 2018).

Employers, for instance, must post mandatory notices in a convenient location about the program and supply claim forms when necessary. Injured employees must obtain all medical treatment, follow-up care, and case management from certified staffs at a qualified workers' compensation facility (McLaren et al., 2018).

State law permits employers to acquire the workers' compensation benefit by four means: exclusive fund operated by the state, competitive fund operated by the state, private insurance, or self-insurance. Four states (see table 2.4) operate an exclusive workers' compensation insurance fund operated by the state, which means that all employers in those states must purchase workers' compensation insurance from the exclusive state fund or become self-insured. The benefits in these states are statutory, which means that state law prescribes benefit amounts and the extent of medical care (Szymendera, 2017).

Although workers' compensation insurance becomes a monopoly in these states, actuaries calculate premiums by employer classifications. Administrative costs in an exclusive fund arrangement remain low because the state does not market the program nor issue renewal policies (Szymendera, 2017).

Eighteen states (see table 2.4) offer the option of purchasing workers' compensation insurance from a competitive fund operated by the state or a private carrier. A competitive fund operated by the state delivers workers' compensation insurance on the open market without regard to the size of the employer's premium, nature of business, or claim loss history. Most competitive fund arrangements operated by the state pay dividends to policyholders and consistently maintain lower administrative costs than private carriers, although a few studies found that states with competitive funds operated by the state have considerably higher workers' compensation insurance premiums than other insurance options (Szymendera, 2017).

Thirty states plus the District of Columbia legislate that employers must purchase workers' compensation insurance from private insurance carriers or maintain a self-insurance account. State regulations limit the insurer's ability to set premiums and dictate employee benefits. Although mandatory or competitive state insurance generally provides workers' compensation to any employer, private insurers are not compelled to offer insurance in all cases (Szymendera, 2017).

When an insurer believes that an employer is too risky, the carrier may deny a policy to that employer, which causes the high-risk employer difficulty in purchasing coverage. On the other hand, because insurance carriers typically issue annual policies, an employer may opt to change the insurance carrier before the policy's renewal date. Many private carriers bundle insurance by offering additional lines of insurance besides workers' compensation, such as property and/or liability (Szymendera, 2017).

All states except North Dakota and Wyoming permit qualifying employers to fund workers' compensation through self-insurance accounts. Under self-insurance, the employer does not purchase insurance from a state fund or private insurer; instead, the employer holds sufficient assets in reserve to pay mandatory workers' compensation insurance claims. Self-insured employers must be approved by the state, and in some cases, self-insured employers must post bonds to ensure that future benefits will be paid regardless of funds or solvency (Szymendera, 2017). Table 2.4 shows each jurisdiction's means by which a school district may procure workers' compensation insurance.

Premiums for workers' compensation insurance typically relate to the injury risk at the workplace, and actuaries rate a district's risk on a base-rated or experience-rated system. Actuaries, in a base-rated method, rank employer risk classifications based on the specific industry, firm size, and nature of the employees' work. By participating in a state workers' compensation insurance program, group participation by classification allows employers to combine historical experiences with similar employers to predict future losses. Participating in a consortium often results in a lower premium than utilizing a private insurer or self-insurance (Martocchio, 2018).

Actuaries, in an experience-rated system, adjust premiums, according to a workplace's actual claim history relative to the employer classification. When the employer's past losses are less than expected, the employer pays a lower premium in an experience-rated system than the base-rated method (Martocchio, 2018).

The cost of workers' compensation insurance continues to concern school systems. Reducing claim frequency remains the best approach to lower workers' compensation rates. Well-designed employee training in a safety prevention program proves to reduce work injuries and resulting claim expenses.

When an employee injury occurs, immediate administrative actions hold a major impact on the claim outcome and expense because supervisors frequently possess first-hand knowledge about the incident and can initially investigate as well as manage the circumstance. Supervisors also may assist in preventing future claims and recognizing appropriate corrective actions to eliminate unsafe conditions and practices that sustain claims.

Proper selection of medical providers, combined with effective referral procedures and consistent communication, can significantly decrease claim expenses. A cost analysis with clear provisions regarding return-to-work language, case management, and prevention may lower costs. For districts in states that do not oblige employers to participate in a state workers' compensation insurance program, a district may elect to negotiate price quotations to compare prices from insurance carriers (Alvarado & Quinn, 2018).

The selection of an insurance carrier and its broker is critical for a district. Without the advice, advocacy, and leverage of a qualified, professional insurance broker, a district loses the opportunity for a risk management consultant who understands the district's immediate and potential risks and recommends strategies for managing risks (Alvarado & Quinn, 2018).

Table 2.4 Workers' Compensation Insurance Procurement

Jurisdiction	*Exclusive*	*Competitive*	*Private Carrier*	*Self-Insurance*	*Jurisdiction*	*Exclusive*	*Competitive*	*Private Carrier*	*Self-Insurance*
Alabama			X	X	Nebraska			X	X
Alaska			X	X	Nevada			X	X
Arizona			X	X	New Hampshire			X	X
Arkansas			X	X	New Jersey			X	X
California		X	X	X	New Mexico		X	X	X
Colorado		X	X	X	New York		X	X	X
Connecticut			X	X	North Carolina			X	X
Delaware			X	X	North Dakota	X			
Florida			X	X	Ohio	X			X
Georgia			X	X	Oklahoma		X	X	X
Hawaii		X	X	X	Oregon		X	X	X
Idaho		X	X	X	Pennsylvania		X	X	X
Illinois			X	X	Rhode Island		X	X	X
Indiana			X	X	South Carolina		X	X	X
Iowa			X	X	South Dakota			X	X
Kansas			X	X	Tennessee			X	X
Kentucky		X	X	X	Texas		X	X	X
Louisiana		X	X	X	Utah		X	X	X
Maine			X	X	Vermont			X	X
Maryland		X	X	X	Virginia			X	X
Massachusetts			X	X	Washington	X		X	X
Michigan			X	X	Washington, DC			X	X
Minnesota			X	X	West Virginia			X	X
Mississippi			X	X	Wisconsin			X	X
Missouri		X	X	X	Wyoming	X			
Montana		X	X	X	Total[a]	4	18	48[b]	49

Notes: [a]The total does not equal fifty states because most states offer multiple choices for workers' compensation insurance procurement.

[b]Thirty states require districts to provide workers' compensation insurance through a private carrier or self-insurance.

Source: Szymendera (2017).

RISK MANAGEMENT

School officials and districts deliver obliged employee fringe benefits along with asset protections from potential hazards, when executing school affairs. Because perilous events (e.g., floods, fires, active campus shootings, and bus accidents) may arise in a school, a district's monetary loss could cripple a budget.

Risk management programs, linked to a potential mishap or calamitous happening, involve safety plans, security policies, procedural guides, trainings, and insurance protections. As with other fiduciary responsibilities, the school board should clearly direct risk management programs by establishing firm policies and procedures to identify, analyze, assess, and control threats to organizational capital as well as avoid, minimize, and eliminate risks (Alliant Insurance Services, 2019).

School boards should safeguard the district against perils with insurance protections too. School officials should prepare the district for possible disasters, recognize proper actions in crisis, and guard district resources. By possessing a keen understanding of risk management acts and realizing the intricacies of property, liability, and fleet insurances, a school official will be well-equipped to safeguard the district.

School officials secure districts against hazards by electing to acquire insurance from a commercial insurance carrier, risk pool membership, or self-insurance method. Twelve states and the District of Columbia (see table 2.5) mandate that districts procure insurance from a commercial insurance carrier, unless the district employs a self-insurance method. Commercial insurers signify for-profit organizations that provide a wide range of insurance products. Most states allow school districts to procure insurance via a private insurance carrier.

Thirty-eight states allow schools to procure risk insurance in a consortium pool. A risk pool characterizes a group of entities with similar exposures that create, in effect, an insurance consortium. As an alternative to the commercial insurance market, consortium risk pools form with school district and/or governmental entity memberships. State associations for school boards (14 states) and school business officials (one state), private organizations (20 states), and state governments (three states) sponsor and offer comprehensive or limited coverages through a risk pool. Districts in two states (Arkansas and Indiana) have an option of risk pool choices.

State law may permit districts to employ a self-insurance method for risk insurances, although very few school districts actually procure risk insurance in this manner. When choosing to self-insure risk insurance, districts typically purchase reinsurance and/or stop-loss coverage to limit potential losses. Proponents of self-insurance stress lower costs than other insurance options; however, critics point to a district's increased financial liability with such a

Table 2.5 Risk Management Insurance Sources(s) with Associated Website(s)

Jurisdiction[a]	*Insurer Source*	*Risk Pool Website*
Alabama	State School Board Risk Pool	http://www.alabamaschoolboards.org/our-services/risk-management
Alaska	Organization Risk Pool	http://www.akpei.com
Arizona	Organization Risk Pool	https://www.svc.the-trust.org/ (Property and Liability)
Arkansas[b]	State School Board Risk Pool or State Government Risk Pool	https://arsba.org/insurance/ (Property only) https://insurance.arkansas.gov (Property and Fleet)
California[c]	Regional Risk Pools	
Colorado	Organization Risk Pool	https://www.csdsip.org (Property and Liability)
Connecticut	Organization Risk Pool	http://cirma.ccm-ct.org/
Florida	State School Board Risk Pool	https://www.fsbit.net
Georgia	State School Board Risk Pool	https://gsba.com/member-services/risk-management/
Idaho	Organization Risk Pool	https://www.icrmp.org/
Illinois	State School Board Risk Pool	https://www.iasb.com/sponsored/insurance.cfm
Indiana[b]	State Government Risk Pool or Organization Risk Pool	https://www.in.gov/idoi/2353.htm https://www.ipep.com/about-ipep/how-ipep-works.aspx (Workers' Compensation and Liability)
Kansas	State School Board Risk Pool	https://kasb.org/risk-management/property-and-casualty-insurance/
Louisiana	Organization Risk Pool	https://welcome.willis.com/larma/default.aspx
Maine	State School Board Risk Pool	https://www.msmaweb.com (Property and Liability)
Maryland	State School Board Risk Pool	https://www.mabe.org/insurance-programs/mabe-programs
Massachusetts	Organization Risk Pool	https://megawcgroup.com/membership/ (Workers' Compensation)
Michigan	State School Board Risk Pool	http://msip.org (Property, Liability, and Fleet)
Minnesota	State School Board Risk Pool	http://www.mnmsba.org/MSBAIT (Property and Liability)
Missouri	Organization Risk Pool	https://www.musicprogram.org (Property, Liability, and Fleet)
Nebraska	Organization Risk Pool	http://www.alicap.org/
Nevada	Organization Risk Pool	https://poolpact.com/Default.asp
New Hampshire	Organization Risk Pool	https://nhprimex.org/
New Jersey	Organization Risk Pool	https://www.njsig.org/index.php
New York	Organization Risk Pool	https://www.nysir.org/default.aspx
North Carolina	County Commissioners	http://www.ncacc.org/

North Dakota	Organization Risk Pool	http://www.ndirf.com/
Ohio	State School Officials Risk Pool	http://www.ohioschoolplan.org (Property, Liability, and Fleet)
Oklahoma	Organization Risk Pool	https://www.osrmt.org (Property, Liability, and Fleet)
Oregon	State Government Risk Pool	http://pace.osba.org (Property, Liability, and Fleet)
South Carolina	State School Board Risk Pool	http://scsba.org/scsbit (Property and Liability)
South Dakota	Organization Risk Pool	http://ptasbsd.org (Property and Liability)
Tennessee	Organization Risk Pool	http://www.tnrmt.com (Property and Liability)
Texas	State School Board Risk Pool	https://www.tasbrmf.org (Property, Liability, and Fleet)
Vermont	State School Board Risk Pool	https://www.vsbit.org/
Virginia	Organization Risk Pool	https://www.vrsa.us/
Washington	Organization Risk Pool	http://siaw.us (Property, Liability, and Fleet)
Wyoming	State School Board Risk Pool	http://www.wsba-wy.org (Property and Liability)

Notes: [a]The table does not list Delaware, Hawaii, Iowa, Kentucky, Mississippi, Montana, New Mexico, Pennsylvania, Rhode Island, Utah, West Virginia, Wisconsin, and the District of Columbia because districts in these jurisdictions must purchase risk management insurances from commercial insurers of the district's choice.

[b]School districts in Arkansas and Indiana maintain various risk pool options.

[c]California has regional risk pools.

structure (Texas Association of School Boards, 2018). Table 2.5 shows each state's source(s) for risk management insurance.

With numerous options to procure risk insurance, school districts or consortium risk pools employ various tasks to procure risk management insurances. When employing a consortium pool for risk insurances, designated agency staff members typically negotiate with carriers, seek brokers' guidance, establish policy terms and conditions, and evaluate as well as select carriers. School officials, on the other hand, who independently choose to purchase risk insurance for their districts may directly contact an insurer. School administrators or CFOs are strongly advised to attract interest by securing price quotations to ensure a fair price from the current carrier or compare prices among insurers (Texas Association of School Boards, 2018).

Employing an insurance broker to advise the district, write bid specifications, and evaluate proposals may prove valuable. Considerations for insurance carrier selection should include the premium payments, deductible rates, coverages, exclusions, and aggregate along with occurrence limits.

As a caution, school administrators should be wary of lowball quotes in which the insurance company representative offers services at an unusually low rate, and then after that first year, the carrier markedly raises the premium. Nevertheless, changing insurance companies should be seamless with regard to exposure and coverages. To avoid lowball quotes, school officials should thoroughly investigate the company's premium history from other districts (Texas Association of School Boards, 2018).

A risk insurance policy represents a binding legal contract with very specific terms and assurances for the insurance carrier and policyholder (e.g., district). Each policy typically contains a declaration page that identifies the policyholder, district address, policy period, and deductible amount (Alliant Insurance Services, 2019).

The policy should also explain coverages, conditions, limitations, and exclusions, which may be detailed as endorsements. An endorsement refers to an amendment or addition to an existing insurance policy that changes the terms or scope of the original policy, including additions, deletions, or exclusions. The policy period usually functions for a six- or twelve-month period and may be automatically renewed; however, the insurer or policyholder may cancel or nonrenew a policy at any time.

The insurer may cancel a policy during the policy period for a premium nonpayment or an unexpected risk. The policyholder may nonrenew a policy at the contract's expiration or cancel a policy during the policy period for an insurer's nonperformance.

Insurance encompasses uncertainty, and premium rates usually fluctuate by actual and estimated claim losses due to local, state, or national calamities. When a disaster strikes, attendant costs (e.g., labor, construction materials, and insurance claims) rise; therefore, insurance actuaries factor these events into future policyholder premiums.

When premiums remain sufficient to shield insurers' claims against local, state, and/or national disasters, then district premiums may not increase. When premium sums do not cover the claims in a year, however, a district's annual premium will most likely increase.

One insurance carrier may offer a bundled set of insurances (e.g., commercial property, general liability, personal liability, workers' compensation, and fleet). The Ohio School Plan (2019), for example, governed by the Ohio school business officials' association, offers the following menu of product coverages—property, criminal and violent acts, general liability, cybersecurity, environmental (i.e., air quality) incidents, personal (i.e., errors and omissions) liability, fiduciary liability (i.e., employee bonding), and fleet liability.

According to King and Bracy (2019), crisis planning and management become the guiding actions to direct prospective and actual events due to school security risks. In the event of an incident, district administrators should prepare for a myriad of possible scenarios. Crisis planning may be as simple as conducting drills to much more elaborate involvements. For example, when a shooting occurs on school property, disaster management is in maximum overdrive.

A well-written crisis management plan should include four phases:

- mitigation and prevention, which are the district and school personnel's actions to avoid incidents;
- preparedness, which include planning activities and practice in the event of potential property damage, personal injury, or school fleet accident;
- response, meaning the actual proceedings during an instance; and
- recovery, pertaining to actions in returning to normal operation (King & Bracy, 2019).

Property Insurance

Property insurance traces its origin to early marine trading days with dangers due to piracy and storms. Fire insurance evolved in the United States by modeling British practices that occurred after the 1666 Great London Fire (Johnson, 2019).

For today's school districts, a blanket insurance policy protects the district against direct physical loss or property damage from covered perils. According to Alliant Insurance Services (2019), potential hazards may encompass "acts of God" (e.g., floods, hurricanes, tornados, windstorms, lightning, earthquakes, and hail), vandalism, terrorism, violent acts, and mechanical failures from equipment (e.g., steam boilers, water and liquid petroleum gas tanks, and air conditioning units).

Other equipment covered by property insurance may include: fire detection apparatus; sprinkler, sewer, and security systems; telecommunication instrumentation; refrigeration mechanisms; elevators; and electronic data processing infrastructures and devices (Alliant Insurance Services, 2019).

Property damage endorsements, purchased separately or declared within a blanket policy, may include, exclude, or limit exposure for the following—builder's risk, criminal acts, cybersecurity and breaches, environmental situations, and violent acts (e.g., terrorism and shootings). Builder's risk insurance would be worthwhile, when a district enters into a major building project because the coverage guards the district against physical damage that may occur during renovation and construction (Alliant Insurance Services, 2019).

Criminal coverage shields the district against property damage due to vandalism. Cybersecurity protects against damage to digital assets and data breaches. With an environmental endorsement, for instance, property insurance protects the district against expenses caused by mold or air-quality issues. Violence protection defends against property damage claims related to violent acts (Alliant Insurance Services, 2019).

To prevent and prepare for damage to district property, administrators should be knowledgeable about the district's property insurance policy and periodically inspect, monitor, and maintain the grounds and building systems. School and district leaders should schedule and implement emergency response drills, constantly monitor weather conditions, and support building safety processes.

When property damage occurs, administrators should investigate the incident and report the situation to the appropriate authorities. Each incident involving a potential personal property claim stands unique; therefore, school officials' actions that result from an incident vary widely. To recover from property damage, school officials must have the damage repaired, conduct debriefings with staff and authorities, and contact the insurance carrier for restitution.

The need for commercial property insurance coverages constantly changes due to market conditions, unforeseen occurrences, and potential tragedies. Due to an increasing number of catastrophes in schools, districts must be well insured with appropriate property coverages.

General Liability Insurance

School districts and administrators encounter frequent latent liabilities and exposures emanating from daily operations. General liability insurance (i.e., casualty insurance) covers claims that arise from a district's liability due to personal damage or injury caused by negligence, unintentional acts, or accidents (Alliant Insurance Services, 2019).

General liability insurance endorsements or coverages under a separate policy may include professional liability, fund raising, sexual misconduct and molestation, mass shootings, and volunteer activities, especially for parent-teacher associations and athletic booster clubs. An umbrella/excess liability policy or endorsement delivers additional protection above the normal levels in a general liability policy. Actuaries rate general liability insurance premiums by factoring previous claims' history, market conditions, endorsements, and occurrences along with aggregate limits into the rate formula (Burnside, 2016).

Although a district's liability risks stand infinite, common exposures involve:

- personal injury on school grounds due to hazardous conditions;
- bullying and cyberbullying threats, assaults, active campus shootings, and data breaches;
- personnel misjudgments from inappropriate employee action and neglectful supervision;
- environmental concerns, resulting from mold, sick building syndrome, pollution, and asbestos; and
- employment issues arising from discrimination or wrongful termination (Alliant Insurance Services, 2019).

Based on these exposures, school districts and individual employees may be held legally liable, especially when an employee commits a tortious act (i.e., a civil wrong or tort) against another person that results in an injury or harm. Across the country, district liability emanates from various circumstances, particularly unintentional torts or negligent acts committed by a staff member. Unintentional torts or negligent acts occur when the person fails to exercise a proper standard of care that a reasonably prudent person would exercise in like circumstances. The district and individuals may also be held accountable due to intentional actions, including assault, battery, or defamation (Alexander & Alexander, 2019).

Negligence, a prevalent source of liability, involves accidental injury to another person. When an injured party pursues negligence charges against the district, the claim examines four necessary elements. Court judges affirm claims, when the following elements exist:

- The district administrators and staff have a legal duty to protect other parties (e.g., students, staff, and community) by conforming to a certain standard of care.

- When administrators or staff members fail to meet the standard of care, a breach of duty occurs.
- A proximate cause (i.e., causal relationship between the breach of duty and the actual injury) must be evident.
- The harmed party must sustain an actual injury based on the breach of duty by the school employee (Alexander & Alexander, 2019).

To prevent and prepare for potential personal injury liabilities, administrators should be knowledgeable of the district's general liability insurance provisions. School officials should also periodically conduct building and grounds safety inspections. With employment issues, administrators should be aware of proper practices in hiring, supervising, and terminating staff to avoid litigation (King & Bracy, 2019).

To prepare for liabilities, administrators should retain school facility information (e.g., maps, aerial and ground photos, floor plans, and visual and written inventories), arrange for command posts and staging areas, establish communication procedures, provide staff training (e.g., bullying, child abuse, sexual and physical harassment, and professional responsibilities), and practice for a possible tragedy (King & Bracy, 2019). With prevention, Alexander and Alexander (2019) noted that foreseeability marks the prevention standard. Foreseeability is the administrator's ability to predict harmful or dangerous situations before an incident occurs.

In the response phase regarding a suspected district negligent act or unintentional tort, an administrator must thoroughly investigate the alleged liability claim against the school district, staff, and/or students. The general liability insurer should be immediately contacted to investigate the incident and reimburse the injured party, when the insurer deems the district and/or employees liable.

When a complainant files a claim against the school district for improperly performing in a cyberbullying or other libelous situation, the district attorney should represent the school. If the school district loses the case and remains liable, the general liability insurer should generate restitution based on the policy guidelines. In suspected cyberbullying, sexting, or bullying incidents, the school administrator should immediately investigate allegations to avoid a possible deliberate indifference claim and execute appropriate actions (Alexander & Alexander, 2019).

Following all tortious acts and neglectful incidents in the recovery phase, the staff should identify follow-up interventions, conduct debriefings with the staff and first responders, monitor stakeholders' reactions to the calamity, reflect on the incident, correct uncovered errors, and contact the school attorney and insurance carrier. Administrators, above all, should be steadfast in their actions to prevent, prepare, respond, and recover from tortious and neglectful incidents.

In a sexting case at a suburban Cincinnati, Ohio, high school, a student hung herself after relentless and hateful taunting by classmates. The parents sued the Sycamore Community School Board of Education and the resource officer, individually. The lawsuit claimed deliberate indifference to sexual harassment under Title IX. The parents alleged that the school and the school resource officer did not help their daughter overcome the harassment. The parties reached a $154,000 settlement for the family and $66,000 in legal fees (Brookshire, 2015).

Fleet Insurance

State law typically obligates school districts to possess fleet and automobile insurance on buses, cars, and other moving vehicles owned by the district, and these laws often set minimum coverage limits. Similar to a personal vehicle insurance policy, a fleet insurance policy generally contains the following coverages—collision, comprehension, bodily injury, property damage, medical, no-fault, and uninsured/underinsured motorist (New Jersey Department of Education, 2016).

Collision coverage, subject to deductible costs, protects damage to district vehicles that result from a collision with another vehicle or object. Comprehensive coverage, subject to deductible as well, indemnifies damage incurred to vehicles from losses other than by collision, such as fire, theft, vandalism, and glass breakage (New Jersey Department of Education, 2016).

Bodily injury liability coverage shields the district against expenses from bodily injury or death sustained during a crash caused by a district driver. Medical coverage safeguards the district against medical expenses in the event of an accident regardless of fault. Property damage liability safeguards the district against damage to another's property. The uninsured/underinsured motorist provision defends the district against damage instigated by an uninsured/underinsured motorist (New Jersey Department of Education, 2016).

Although boards of education may protect vehicles with coverage beyond the state minimum, Delaware, like many other states, requires that all buses operated by any person under contract with a school district or charter school that transports students be covered by minimum insurance coverages.

The Delaware statute, originally written in 1935 and revised in 1953, remains in force today with minimum coverages consisting of

- bodily injury and property damage with a combined single limit of $1 million,

- personal injury protection coverage of $100,000 per occurrence and $300,000 aggregate,
- medical payment coverage of $2,000 per person, and
- uninsured motorist coverage of $300,000 (Transportation of Pupils, 1953).

To prepare for a bus accident, school administrators should plan in the same way as other conceivable emergencies with four response cycles—prevention, preparedness, response, and recovery. Appropriate prevention actions include understanding the district fleet insurance policy, identifying known driving hazards, conducting and reviewing safety audits, encouraging the staff to provide input about safety issues, and reviewing past accident data to determine vulnerability to certain conditions and kinds of accidents (Kerr & King, 2018).

Communicating bus accident responsibilities in an understandable format via a handbook or code of conduct for all stakeholders ensures student safety in the prevention phase. School officials should also identify and communicate in advance of an accident with all the partners who might be involved in an accident response—administrators, staff, students, parents, emergency medical technicians, law enforcement officers, and media outlets. Practicing bus evacuation and accident drills along with training the staff on proper routines facilitates apt action in the prevention phase (Kerr & King, 2018).

School personnel, in the response phase, must immediately communicate with stakeholders and accurately assess the situation. School administrators, in most cases, should immediately report to the accident scene. Emergency care forms and bus rosters should be available (Kerr & King, 2018).

When arriving at the scene, school officials should follow the emergency medical technicians and police officers' directions. School administrators should identify all students, monitor emergency first aid treatment at the scene, and assess the disposition of all injuries before transporting the injured parties to the hospital or releasing students to their parents. School officials should document the accident scene through reports and pictures. A school administrator must advise the school bus driver that he or she must submit to an alcohol and drug test, as required by law (Kerr & King, 2018).

The goal of the recovery phase is to return as quickly as possible to normal operations. Immediately after the accident, the damaged vehicle should be towed to a determined location and repaired when possible. School officials should check on injured and hospitalized students. A specified school official must contact the fleet insurer regarding the accident and file a claim. Other recovery actions include assessing the emotional impact of an accident on students, identifying and implementing follow-up interventions for students and staff, conducting debriefings, and revising accident plans when necessary (Kerr & King, 2018).

In 2018, a Norman, Oklahoma, school bus driver lost control of a bus, and the bus rolled multiple times. Twenty-five students and three faculty members were on board with five students and two faculty members hospitalized. All 28 people on board were injured to some degree (Sweetman, 2018).

The district, through the Oklahoma Schools Risk Management Trust, possessed the state's legal minimum insurance requirement of $1 million single occurrence limit with each individual insured to a maximum of $125,000. Norman Public Schools officials accepted full liability for the accident and exhausted the $1 million limit. A lawsuit has been filed, and the court will appoint an individual to decide the allocation of each claim's damages until depleting the policy limit. Parents may elect to file additional liability claims against the school (Sweetman, 2018).

SUMMARY

School districts provide a wide range of employee benefits, and these fringe benefits represent important aspects of an eminent compensation package to attract and retain quality employees. All district employees should be aware of their benefits, and school administrators must be knowledgeable about these benefits due to the potential drain on the budget.

To control and contain costs without cutting appropriate health care, eight cost drivers include:

- aging population and progressing chronic diseases;
- advancing medical technology, including pharmaceutical drugs;
- increasing expenses due to limited cost-sharing features in programs;
- challenging administrative complexity and paperwork;
- supplying the professional health workforce in underserved area and occupation shortages;
- consolidating insurers that cause an imbalance in market power;
- lacking transparency in costs; and
- mounting fraud and abuse cases (Hodgin, 2019).

Aside from the loss of life and pain that a deadly shooting inflicts on a school district and community, campus shootings also have a financial drain on district resources that can devastate a school and community. After a school catastrophe, public attention usually focuses on the personal aftershock of the horrific event, and discussions ensue about procedures to prevent another such incident.

School officials, unfortunately, must handle the tragedy from a personal level and manage the incident from a risk management perspective too. At

Columbine High School in Littleton, Colorado, for instance, 13 people were killed and 20 more injured. The total cost from the 1999 shooting was roughly $50 million (Delgadillo, 2018).

At Sandy Hook Elementary in 2012, a mass shooter killed 28 people and injured two. To help rebuild the school, Connecticut granted the city of Newtown $50 million. At a high school in Parkland, Florida, in 2018, 17 people were killed and more than a dozen injured. The school district intends to demolish and rebuild a part of the school building, which will cost millions of dollars (Delgadillo, 2018).

Upon restoring order and managing a disaster scene, school personnel must react to the situation by taking appropriate steps to address student challenges, staff issues, and building concerns. An injured staff member in a school shooting, for example, may participate in the workers' compensation program through mandated compliances. The workers' compensation program, more than likely, would provide an injured staff member with necessary healthcare treatments, but when this is not the case, the district's group medical program may be impacted. With staff loss of life, the school's group life insurance would provide survivor benefits for the loved one's family, and workers' compensation would also compensate survivors.

Staff members must ready the building for normal operations after the attack. The cleanup could incur unforeseen expenses beyond the property insurance policy limit. When a violent death occurs in a school, federal regulations deem all bodily fluids to be biohazardous; thus, any blood or tissue at a crime scene is a potentially infectious substance. To ensure safe conditions, specially trained personnel must dispose of any biohazardous material that resulted from the violent act.

When an injury of any kind occurs at a school, parents or students may file a lawsuit against the school board, administration, and staff. When the school board authorizes a teacher to carry a firearm in the classroom or building, potential liabilities may include personal claims that result from a loss, stolen, or accidentally/intentionally discharged firearm.

Other potential liability with authorized armed staff may result from a teacher's threat to use a firearm, injuries to the teacher in the course of training or firearm discharge, or the discharge of a firearm at a perceived threat, intruder, colleague, or administrator. The firing at a perceived threat that accidentally hits an innocent third party may result in a liability case against the school and individual.

Another concern is whether school liability insurance would or would not protect the district against claims related to fired weapons from authorized armed employees in the school. Besides regular liability insurance premium increases, the district workers' compensation premium expense could also increase, when an employer experiences an employee injury or death.

Although most school officials do not enter the profession to become insurance gurus, having a working knowledge of the district's benefit programs and risk insurances remains essential. Some superintendents believe that they do not need to be aware of the intricacies of the district's benefit programs and risk insurances, and this management responsibility may be delegated to others, such as the business manager or CFO. Superintendents, however, should be reminded that they are accountable for the district's entire business operation, and when issues arise, the "buck stops at the organization's top." With comprehension, school administrators have a better chance of managing the financial side of these protections and containing costs.

PROJECTS

1. Critique your district's employee health insurance plan document, distinguish cost-sharing provisions along with coverage limitations, and compare findings with another district's plan.
2. Participate in a group health insurance committee, analyze insurance utilization data, and devise provisions for district/employee cost savings without harming the integrity of the program.
3. When the jurisdiction allows collective bargaining, participate in the negotiations of employee benefits.
4. Explore your jurisdiction's Employee Relations Board data to discover school district data:
    a. health insurance administrative structures,
    b. health insurance plan delivery designs,
    c. health insurance consortium participation,
    d. average health plan premiums,
    e. average deductible,
    f. prescription drug coverage participation,
    g. vision coverage participation, and
    h. dental coverage participation.
5. Stay current on healthcare issues at the local, jurisdiction, and national levels and share findings with colleagues.
6. Distinguish between pension assurances plus professional liability, unemployment, workers' compensation, property, general liability and fleet insurances and detect opportunities to save money for a school district in each program.
7. Conduct a walk-through of a school building and inspect the premises for hazardous conditions.

Chapter 3

Funding Capital Investments

OBJECTIVES

After reading this chapter, you should be able to

- ✓ assess a district's existing capital assets and prioritize needs (NELP 3.1, 4.1, 6.1, 6.2, 7.3, 7.4);
- ✓ compare and contrast a district's capital funding opportunities (NELP 5.3, 6.1, 6.2, 7.3, 7.4);
- ✓ describe the processes that a jurisdiction exercises to fund fixed assets, school construction, and building renovations (NELP 5.3, 6.1, 6.2, 7.3, 7.4); and
- ✓ develop a preliminary capital budget and apply for a capital project grant (NELP 5.3, 6.1, 6.2, 7.3, 7.4).

Districts across the United States, on average, spend 2% of their entire budget for capital outlay to acquire land; modernize, modify, and upgrade (i.e., retrofit) buildings; construct new structures; build additions; and pay debt interest (McFarland et al., 2019). Technology, furnishings, vehicles, equipment, machinery, architect and engineer services, building demolition, and major maintenance usually define fixed capital assets, although the law in each state and the District of Columbia (i.e., jurisdictions) describe specific definitions. Some jurisdictions additionally classify interest on debt and government loan repayment as capital outlay (Cornman, Zhou, Howell, & Young, 2018).

Considering capital investments, expenditures may embody an unevenness in spending, combined with substantial planning. School renovation, for instance, may cost a district millions of dollars in one year, but expenditures may be minimal in other years (Schilling & Tomal, 2019).

Major renovation and new construction projects, therefore, greatly disrupt the district operation. Generally, the CFO separately appropriates the capital project budget from the general fund budget because extensive capital projects are often periodic, costly expenditures. The general fund, on the other hand, primarily accounts for unrestricted local and state sources and occasionally itemizes spending for minor equipment repairs, less expansive building modifications, technology hardware, green solutions, or security measures (Schilling & Tomal, 2019).

Table 3.1 illustrates national total capital outlay expenditures, by category, at primary and secondary public schools and corresponding percentages in fiscal year 2017, which is the most current U.S. Department of Education data at the time of publication.

Table 3.1 National Capital Outlay Expenditures and Percentages by Category, 2017

Category	*Expenditure*	*Capital Outlay Percentage*
Construction	$49,219,222	78.3%
Land	$3,700,064	5.9%
Instructional Equipment	$2,031,676	3.2%
Other Equipment	$7,834,026	12.5%
Total Capital Expenses	$62,784,988	99.9%[a]
Debt Interest	$17,990,172	Not Counted in Sum

Note: [a]The sum of average percentages does not equal 100% due to rounding.

Source: U.S. Census Bureau (2019a).

The United States, unfortunately, underinvests in school buildings. An annual estimated deficit of $38 billion subsists to improve public school buildings with 24% of the structures across the country rated in poor or fair condition (American Society of Civil Engineers, 2017). To exacerbate this problem, sharp inequities exist between districts with a strong tax base and property-poor schools because a community's fiscal capacity heavily influences a district's capital spending (Richmond, 2019).

CAPITAL FINANCE OPTIONS

To fund traditional public schools' capital expenditures throughout the United States, local funding, on average, assumes the heftiest burden because communities financed 82% of all capital projects from 1994 to 2013. States averaged

17.8% of primary and secondary public school facilities' capital investments during that time. Due to the federal government's position (i.e., Tenth Amendment), federal sources funded a mere 0.2% of traditional public schools' capital needs (Filardo, 2016). *State of Our Schools: America's K–12 Facilities* (Filardo, 2016), the most thorough account of America's K–12 facilities at the time of publication, is a joint project of the National Council on School Facilities, 21st Century School Fund, and the Center for Green Schools.

Filardo (2016) indicated that 12 states (see table 3.2) did not earmark any direct funding to public schools for capital spending from 1994 to 2013. Seven states designated only a fraction (1% to 9%) of the total districts' capital spending; nine states apportioned between 10% and 25%; eight states awarded between 26% and 49%; five states allotted over 50% of districts' entire capital expenses during 1994–2013. Hawaii allocated 100% of all schools' capital spending. Table 3.2 shows the average percentages of local and state capital support, by state, for primary and secondary public school districts.

Table 3.2 Local and State Capital Support for Public School Districts, 1994–2013[a]

State[b]	*Local Percentage*	*State Percentage*	*State[b]*	*Local Percentage*	*State Percentage*
Alabama	78	22	Maryland	74	26
Alaska	63	37	Massachusetts	33	67
Arizona	79	21	Minnesota	78	22
Arkansas	88	12	Mississippi	98	2
California	72	28	Montana	99	1
Colorado	97	3	New Hampshire	81	19
Connecticut	43	57	New Jersey	68	32
Delaware	43	57	New Mexico	80	20
Florida	85	15	New York	64	36
Georgia	88	12	North Carolina	92	8
Hawaii	0	100	North Dakota	98	2
Illinois[c]	96	4	Rhode Island	22	78
Iowa[c]	65	35	South Carolina	92	8
Kansas	92	8	Washington	86	14
Kentucky	67	33	Wyoming	37	63
Maine	72	28			

Notes: [a]The table shows the most available school capital support data at the time of publication and does not include the District of Columbia because that government body did not report data.

[b]The table does not list Idaho, Indiana, Louisiana, Michigan, Missouri, Nebraska, Nevada, Oklahoma, Oregon, South Dakota, Tennessee, and Wisconsin because these states did not provide any state support for district capital expenses.

[c]The state governments in Iowa and Illinois have not funded school construction since 2002 and 2013, respectively.

Source: Filardo (2016).

With such a reliance on local funding, school districts implement one or more of the following approaches to finance capital needs: cash reserves (i.e., pay-as-you-go plans), sinking funds (i.e., capital projects), and/or general obligation as well as revenue bonds (Brimley et al., 2020).

By applying judicious budgeting and conservative purchasing practices, districts may accumulate dollars from unrestricted local and state revenue sources for capital outlay. School officials may transfer general fund dollars into a capital project fund for the express purpose of financing capital outlay expenses; however, restricted capital project fund monies may not be transferred into the general fund (Brimley et al., 2020).

By using cash surpluses, the pay-as-you-go plan spreads expenditures over a period of time, implements simple procedures for financing ventures, and avoids debt interest. With revenues in reserve, administrators may become more consciously aware of spending; however, saving money for capital endeavors may pit one spending priority over others (Brimley et al., 2020).

Very affluent and large districts normally characterize the schools most capable of implementing cash reserve initiatives because low-wealth and small districts typically struggle to pay essential budgetary obligations. Using cash deposits generally remains a frequent payment plan for less expensive capital outlay expenditures (Brimley et al., 2020; Wood, Thompson, & Crampton, 2019).

Similar to cash reserves, district officials may choose to establish a capital project sinking fund. When instituting a sinking fund, district administrators and the staff deposit excess cash into a designated account until sufficient funds are available to pay for a capital project. After amassing money, school officials may spend sinking funds immediately without an approved referendum by the voters. This payment mechanism also avoids interest charges on debt (Brimley et al., 2020).

Permanent improvement levies in Ohio may establish a sinking fund and finance fixed assets with a life of five or more years. Passing a permanent improvement levy typically inaugurates capital projects. With voter approval, this type of referendum allows a district to levy a property tax millage for a set time (i.e., not to exceed 10 years) with the sole purpose of financing capital endeavors. Voters may renew a permanent improvement levy, when the previous levy expires. School officials cannot expend permanent improvement levy dollars for operating expenses, transfer proceeds into the general fund, or allocate monies for debt interest (Ohio School Boards Association, 2018c).

Issuing bonds stands as the most common local practice to meet major capital project needs. State election law legislates school district procedures to qualify bond initiatives, establish election dates, set passage rates (e.g., simple majority or supermajority), and determine district ballot costs. Passing a general obligation bond issue allows the district to build new schools, renovate facilities, purchase fixed assets, and/or exceed the school debt beyond a state's legally protected millage limit (Ballotpedia, 2019).

In order to fund bonds and acquire capital debt, election law in 28 states compels independent school districts to place a bond referendum before the residential electorate. Districts in Arizona, Florida, Minnesota, Montana, Oregon, and Wisconsin may either petition voters before conducting a bond issue or allow voters to petition the district for a bond election (Ballotpedia, 2019).

Colorado, Indiana, and Nevada mandate a petition and remonstrance process to pass a school bond issue. This process allows local property taxpayers to prevent a school construction referendum from being positioned for a residential vote, when more property taxpayers sign a remonstrance against an initiative than taxpayers who favor the proposition. With a positive petition, the residential voters then may approve or deny the bond issue (Ballotpedia, 2019).

For dependent school districts, the parent government's electorate must pass a school bond referendum. Georgia mandates a countywide referendum to pass an initial local sales surtax to secure bonds. After obtaining the initial approval, the county, however, continues to collect increased local sales surtax revenue without voter approval (Ballotpedia, 2019).

Nine states authorize a governing body to approve bond issuance: Alaska, Department of Education; Connecticut, state bond commission; Hawaii, state legislature; Massachusetts, board of alderman; Mississippi, state bond commission; Vermont and New Hampshire, school board; Rhode Island, board of trustees; and North Carolina and Tennessee, county commission. The mayor and city council in the District of Columbia must approve bond issuance (Ballotpedia, 2019).

Local property tax supports bond debt in 42 states; seven states authorize bond debt backed by property tax and/or a local sales surtax approved by the county voters. Six states permit another distinctive tax to support bonds in addition to property or local sales surtax—Alabama, severance; Florida, vehicle property; Maryland, real estate transfer; North Dakota, corporate income; Ohio, local individual income; and Oregon, excise (Ballotpedia, 2019).

Seventeen states have debt limits for bond elections to control revenue increases; therefore, when a school district wants to exceed the limit, election law orders a referendum. In North Carolina, however, a referendum to exceed the debt limit is mandatory, but a community vote is unnecessary for bond issuance under the debt limit because county commissioners sanction such bond requests (Ballotpedia, 2019). To become knowledgeable about a specific state's bond election requirements, click or search for the Ballotpedia website at https://ballotpedia.org/Voting_on_school_bond_and_tax_measures.

After a successful bond election, the district arranges bonding and long-term borrowing. Because construction costs are expensive, most school districts prefer securing long-term debt through a bond sale because bond repayments (i.e., principal and interest) normally extend 20 years or more. To begin the bonding process, the school board selects a bond counsel, a specialized attorney or law firm, to advise the district in advertising, issuing, selling, delivering, and certifying the bonds (Arial, 2019).

Before advertising a competitive bid for a bond sale, the bond counsel gathers recent district financial audit data and acquires a district credit rating from an agency (e.g., Moody's Investment or Standard and Poor's Financial Services). Bond ratings vary from *AAA* to *C* with numerous rating levels in between. The highest rating, *AAA*, indicates that a district possesses a strong capacity to repay incurred debt, whereas a district with a *C* ranking, the lowest score, holds a high probability of debt default (Arial, 2019).

A district should desire a high credit rating because the *AAA* rank results in a lower borrowing interest rate and attracts more bond bids due to a lesser investor risk than a *C* rating. With a district's fiscal information and bond rating, the bond counsel creates a prospectus that describes the issue for prospective investors (Arial, 2019).

After certifying the bond rate and writing the prospectus, the bond counsel prepares and initiates the competitive bid process for the bond sale to underwriters. Competitive bids declare interest rates and maturity dates in proposals. Bond counsel and district officials open and award the bond bids much like other competitive bids, as explained in chapter 1.

Following the board's bid awards, bond counsel has serial bonds printed with differing maturity dates to provide a consistent stream for bond repayment. The state usually verifies the bonds. The district's accumulated principal and interest represent the debt owed to bondholders. The funds become immediately accessible for district investment upon bond sale (Arial, 2019).

Subsequent to the receipt of money generated by the bond sale, districts in some states may reinvest the bond monies and arrange an arbitrage transaction, which refers to a temporary reinvestment of bond proceeds. An arbitrage arrangement typically pays the district a higher investment interest rate than the interest paid by a bank on bond revenue. State law governs a district's ability to reinvest bond revenue through arbitrage, and district leaders should consult with bond counsel before reinvesting bond proceeds in an arbitrage plan (Arial, 2019).

Borrowing interest rates may become lower over a bond issue's lifetime similar to home mortgage interest rates; therefore, a district may refinance outstanding bonds. This refunding action, similar to an individual who remortgages a home loan, may shorten the district's repayment period due to a lower interest rate. When refinancing a bond issue, the public does not have an opportunity to vote in favor or against the act, although the school board must approve the proceeding (Arial, 2019).

Akin to the state operating budget, the capital budget cycle varies by state. Twenty-five states and the District of Columbia (see table 3.3) enact an annual capital budget. Massachusetts does not mandate an annual capital budget, although legislators review and budget a yearly capital investment plan. Twenty-one states ratify a biennial capital budget, and three states concurrently legislate an annual and biennial capital budget (National Association of State Budget Officers, 2014).

Capital Budgeting in the States (National Association of State Budget Officers, 2014) is the most current report of capital budgeting processes by states at the time of publication. According to an official at the National Association of State Budget Officers, the organization does not update the publication very often because the information does not change much over time (B. Sigritz, personal communication, September 17, 2019).

Thirty-two state legislatures and the mayor with the city council in the District of Columbia (see table 3.3) control a jurisdiction's public capital investment funding with a distinct capital budget. Eighteen states coordinate the capital budget within the operating budget (National Association of State Budget Officers, 2014). Table 3.3 shows each jurisdiction's capital budget cycle with specific distinctions between a separate capital budget or within the operating budget.

Similar to state budgets for school operating funds, capital budgets fell sharply after the 2008 recession in most states. Thirty-seven states reduced capital budgets relative to inflation for primary and secondary public schools by 31% after the 2008 fiscal year, representing a national $23 billion cut in funding. Six states sliced capital spending by more than half (Leachman, Masterson, & Figueroa, 2017).

The National Association of State Budget Officers (2018) noted that states estimated a 3.1% capital spending growth in 2018 and reported an actual 5% growth in 2017. While state capital spending can fluctuate from year to year, the historical average level of growth since 1991 is 4.1%.

States, on average, estimated 64.1% of their entire capital spending on transportation (e.g., maintenance and expansion) for the 2018 fiscal year. Corrections (e.g., prisons and highway patrol) obtained 15.6% of the total spent; public higher education institutions, 10.8%; primary and secondary public schools, 2.7%; environmental (e.g., water and sewage treatment plants), 5.3%; housing, 1%; and all others (e.g., parks, hospitals, and other state facilities), 14.8% (National Association of State Budget Officers, 2018).

Each state defines fixed assets differently. Conventional references in associated state statutes signify fixed assets as capital construction in 50 states; land acquisition, 47 states; equipment, 41 states; and information technology,

Table 3.3 Capital Budget Cycle with Specific Distinctions[a]

	Specific Distinction					Specific Distinction			
Jurisdiction	*Annual Budget*	*Biennial Budget*	*Separate Capital Budget*	*Operating Budget*	*Jurisdiction*	*Annual Budget*	*Biennial Budget*	*Separate Capital Budget*	*Operating Budget*
Alabama	X			X	Nebraska		X	X	
Alaska	X		X		Nevada		X	X	
Arizona	X		X		New Hampshire		X	X	
Arkansas		X	X		New Jersey	X			X
California	X			X	New Mexico	X		X	
Colorado	X		X		New York	X		X	
Connecticut		X	X		North Carolina		X		X
Delaware	X		X		North Dakota		X		X
Florida	X		X		Ohio		X	X	
Georgia	X			X	Oklahoma	X		X	
Hawaii		X		X	Oregon		X	X	
Idaho	X			X	Pennsylvania	X		X	
Illinois	X		X		Rhode Island	X		X	
Indiana		X		X	South Carolina	X			X
Iowa[b]	X	X		X	South Dakota	X		X	
Kansas[b]	X	X		X	Tennessee	X		X	
Kentucky		X	X		Texas		X		X
Louisiana	X		X		Utah	X		X	
Maine		X		X	Vermont		X	X	
Maryland	X		X		Virginia[b]	X	X		X
Massachusetts[c]	NA		X		Washington		X	X	
Michigan	X			X	Washington, DC	X		X	
Minnesota		X	X		West Virginia	X			X
Mississippi	X		X		Wisconsin		X	X	
Missouri		X		X	Wyoming		X	X	
Montana		X	X		Total[d]	29	24	33	18

Notes: [a]The data for this table from *Capital Budgeting in the States* is the most current report of capital budgeting by state at the time of publication.

[c]Iowa, Kansas, and Virginia concurrently enact annual and biennial capital funds within the operating budget.

[c]The state does not require an annual capital budget; however, legislators yearly review and budget the capital investment plan.

[d]Because the table lists the District of Columbia and three states in more than one group, the jurisdiction total does not equal fifty-one.

Source: National Association of State Budget Officers (2014).

29 states. To see specific state fixed asset definitions, life spans, approved expenditure items, and treatment of maintenance and repairs, click or search for the National Association of State Budget Officers website at https://www.nasbo.org/mainsite/reports-data/capital-budgeting-in-the-states, seek the full report, and look at table 2.1 in *Capital Spending in the States*.

The *2018 State Expenditure Report* by the National Association of State Budget Officers (2018) collected and reported specific state primary and secondary education capital expenditures for the first time in this publication. According to this document, which is the most current capital expenditure data at the time of publication, 24 states separately counted capital expenditures for primary and secondary education, while the remaining states did not convey state capital expenditures for school districts.

State funding for capital projects derives from varying state sources with states occasionally employing a number of alternatives. Twenty-two states (see table 3.4) issued a general obligation (GO) or revenue bond (RB) to support capital funding as a sole source or in conjunction with other sources. Twenty states designated the state's operating budget with general fund appropriations (GFA) for specific capital outlay expenditures (National Association of State Budget Officers, 2018).

Ten states appropriated lottery proceeds (LoP) within the general fund for capital expenses; five states dedicated state sales tax revenue (DSST) for school facilities funding. Twenty-one states targeted other designated sources (ODS) for capital construction, such as tax on cigarettes, wholesale marijuana, utility and communications, coal and timber severance, individual and corporate income, and real estate transfer (Colorado Department of Education, 2019; National Association of State Budget Officers, 2018).

Proceeds from horse racetrack-casino licensing fees in Ohio; fines and unclaimed property in Virginia and Indiana; fines, forfeitures, and public land sales in Wisconsin; and mineral royalties in Wyoming financed public school construction programs. Four states did not assist school districts in constructing public school facilities (National Association of State Budget Officers, 2018). Table 3.4 shows the state-by-state capital funding sources by category.

After passing a local bond referendum and issuing bonds, a district may attempt to secure state construction or renovation funds. A number of states oblige districts to pass a local bond referendum before granting state aid for school construction. District voters in Ohio, for instance, must approve a bond issue backed by property tax in conjunction with a 0.5 mill permanent improvement levy to maintain the new building before collecting state facility funds (Ohio School Facilities Commission, 2019).

States authorize funding oversight responsibility to public agencies, quasi-public corporations, or boards assigned by the state. These organizations

Table 3.4 Capital Funding Sources by Category, FY 2017[a]

State[b]	*GO/RB*	*GFA*	*LoP*	*DSST*	*ODS*	*State[b]*	*GO/RB*	*GFA*	*LoP*	*DSST*	*ODS*
Alabama	$60 M	$2 M			$178 M	Mississippi	$5 M			X	
Alaska		$11 M			$7 M (Cigarette Tax)	Missouri	$1 M				$1 M (Gambling)
Arizona		$24 M				Montana		X			
Arkansas		X				New Hampshire	$12 M			X	
California	X					New Jersey		$1 M	X		$1 M
Colorado[c]		$4 M			Marijuana and Real Estate Transfer Tax	New Mexico	$224 M		X		
Connecticut	$278 M					New York	$50 M	X	X	$4 M	
Delaware	X					North Carolina		$6 M	X		Corporate Income Tax
Florida	X				Utility Tax and Vehicle License fees	North Dakota					Coal Severance Tax
Georgia	$252 M					Ohio	$227 M				$60 M (Racetrack-casino Licensing Fees)
Hawaii	X				Income Tax	Oregon		X	X		
Idaho			X			Pennsylvania		X			
Illinois	$60 M				$13 M	Rhode Island	$3 M	X			$3 M
Indiana					Unclaimed Property	South Carolina		$15 M		X	$7 M
Iowa					Gambling Profits	Tennessee		X			
Kansas		X				Texas		X	X		
Kentucky		X			$4 M	Utah	$14 M				$22 M (Income Tax)
Louisiana		X				Vermont	X				
Maine		X				Virginia			X		Fines, Unclaimed Property
Maryland	$337 M					Washington	$286 M		X		$41 M (Severance, Real Estate Transfer Tax)

Massachusetts	$18 M	X	West Virginia	$1 M	X	
Michigan	X		Wisconsin			Fines, Forfeitures, and Public Land Sales
Minnesota	$2 M		Wyoming			Mineral Royalties

Notes: [a]The National Association of State Budget Officers (2018) reported twenty-four states' actual capital spending, by category, in the 2017 fiscal year.

[b]The table does not list Nebraska, Nevada, Oklahoma, and South Dakota because these states have no role in school capital outlay. The District of Columbia is not listed because that jurisdiction did not report data.

[c]Beginning in 2018, the Colorado legislature amended the state constitution to dedicate the first $40 million in revenue from excise taxes on wholesale marijuana sales for new school constructions or building renovations. M, million.

Sources: Colorado Department of Education (2019) and National Association of State Budget Officers (2018).

administer state funding, approve master facility plans, sanction construction, and offer technical advice on building standards.

To assist districts with funding, planning, and constructing school facilities, 32 state departments of education (see table 3.5) are contact points. The state department of education in 15 of these 32 states, however, shares oversight tasks with other governmental organizations.

Specific staff members at the California Department of Education, for example, guide facility planning and approve state assistance in conjunction with the State Allocation Board staff, while the assigned Office of Public School Construction employees implement the school facility program, verify that applicant school districts meet the criteria for the requested funding, and disburse funds. Division of the State Architect representatives review construction plans and validate building code compliance (California Office of Public School Construction, 2019).

Ten states and the District of Columbia authorize a distinct agency devoid from the state department of education to accept and approve state monies. These bodies also assist and direct districts in the renovation and construction process.

The Ohio Facility Construction Commission (OFCC) staff, for example, manages and assigns public construction funding for elementary and secondary schools, state higher education institutions, and other state agencies. The OFCC staff also approves state funding applications and administers building plans for the projects (Ohio School Facilities Commission, 2019).

Eighteen states involve more than one agency in assigning state funds and guiding the construction process. The department of education staffs in seven states administer funding, but another state agency offers guidance. A board assigned by the state in five states directs the renovation and construction process. An advisory committee in five states delivers policy and funding recommendations. Members in state legislatures for five states supervise school facility funding requests. Table 3.5 lists construction oversight organization(s) by jurisdiction.

Programs fundable by statute are the predominant distribution method for states to allot monies for new construction or major renovation. To distribute these funds to districts, states utilize equalized project or unequalized project applications, debt service, loan, state bond guarantee programs, or categorical aid in conjunction with the state's basic aid program (Wood et al., 2019).

Fifteen states distribute state construction aid by application that weighs equalizing factors (e.g., district wealth) among requests (see table 3.6). The state allocation typically is inversely proportionate to a district's fiscal capacity (i.e., per-pupil property valuation); thereby, low-wealth districts obtain

Table 3.5 Construction Oversight Organization(s) with Associated Website[a]

Oversight	*Jurisdiction[b]*	*Associated Website*
Department of Education	Alabama,	https://www.alsde.edu/sec/sarch/Pages/home.aspx
	Alaska,	https://education.alaska.gov/facilities/facilitiescip
	Arkansas,	http://arkansasfacilities.arkansas.gov/facilities/construction
	California,	http://www.calschoolconstruction.dgs.ca.gov
	Colorado,	https://www.cde.state.co.us/cdefinance/capconstmain
	Connecticut,	http://portal.ct.gov/DAS/Office-of-School-Construction-Grants/Office-of-School-Construction-Grants-Policies-and-Memos
	Delaware,	https://dfm.delaware.gov/profsrv/proj-schools.shtml
	Florida,	http://www.fldoe.org/finance/edual-facilities
	Georgia,	http://www.gadoe.org/FinanceandBusinessOperations/FacilitiesServices/Pages/default.aspx
	Hawaii,	http://www.hawaiipublicschools.org/ConnectWithUsOrganization/SchoolFacilities/Pages/home.aspx
	Illinois,	https://www.isbe.net/Pages/School-Construction.aspx, however, the state has not provided any funding since 2013
	Kansas,	http://www.ksde.org/Agency/Fiscal-and-Administrative-Services/School-Finance/Guidelines-and-Manuals/Qualified-School-Construction-Bonds
	Kentucky,	https://education.ky.gov/districts/fac/Pages/Construction.aspx
	Maine,	http://www.maine.gov/doe/facilities/construction/process-summary.html
	Minnesota,	https://education.mn.gov/MDE/dse/schfin/fac/cons/
	Mississippi,	http://www.mde.k12.ms.us/MBE/manual/policy-5100-mississippi-adequate-education-capital-improvement-section
	Montana,	http://leg.mt.gov/content/Committees/Interim/2015-2016/School-Funding/Meetings/Apr-2016/Facilities-options.pdf
	New Hampshire,	https://www.education.nh.gov/program/school_approval/documents/ed321-2-2-17.pdf
	New Jersey,	https://www.state.nj.us/education/facilities/laws/act_summ.shtml
	New Mexico,	http://www.nmpsfa.org/legacy/redesign/pscoc.html
	New York,	http://www.nmpsfa.org/legacy/redesign/pscoc.html
	North Carolina,	https://stateaid.nysed.gov/build/building_info.htm

Continued

Table 3.5 (Continued)

Oversight	*Jurisdiction*[b]	*Associated Website*
	North Dakota,	https://www.ncleg.net/PED/Reports/documents/SchoolConstruction/School_Construction_Report.pdf
	Oregon,	https://www.nd.gov/dpi/SchoolStaff/SchoolFinance/SchoolConstruction/NDDPIConstructionLoanProgram/
	Pennsylvania,	https://www.oregon.gov/ode/schools-and-districts/grants/Pages/K-12-School-Funding-Information.aspx
	Rhode Island,	http://www.education.pa.gov/Teachers%20%20Administrators/School%20Construction%20and%20Facilities/Pages/Reimbursable-Projects.aspx
	South Carolina,	http://www.ride.ri.gov/FundingFinance/SchoolBuildingAuthority/NecessityofSchoolConstruction.aspx
	Texas,	https://ed.sc.gov/districts-schools/school-planning-building/
	Utah,	https://tea.texas.gov/Finance_and_Grants/State_Funding/Facilities_Funding_and_Standards/Facilities_Funding_and_Standards/
	Vermont,	https://www.schools.utah.gov/financialoperations/formsapplications
	Virginia,	http://education.vermont.gov/vermont-schools/school-operations/public-schools/facilities-construction
	Washington	https://www.trs.virginia.gov/Boards-Authorities/Virginia-Public-School-Authority
		http://www.k12.wa.us/SchFacilities/Programs/SchoolConstructionProjects.aspx
Other State Agency	Alabama,	https://www.alsde.edu/sec/sarch/Pages/home.aspx
	California,	http://www.calschoolconstruction.dgs.ca.gov
	Illinois,	https://www.isbe.net/Pages/School-Construction.aspx, however, no funds have been allocated since 2013
	Maryland,	http://www.pscp.state.md.us/APG/FIN%20Original%20APG%20Revised%206-6-17.pdf
	North Dakota,	https://www.nd.gov/dpi/SchoolStaff/SchoolFinance/SchoolConstruction/NDDPIConstructionLoanProgram/
	Virginia	https://www.trs.virginia.gov/Boards-Authorities/Virginia-Public-School-Authority

Stand-alone Agency	Arizona,	https://sfb.az.gov/
	Kentucky,	https://education.ky.gov/districts/fac/Pages/Construction.aspx
	Massachusetts,	http://www.massschoolbuildings.org/
	Michigan,	No specific funds nor guidance
	New Jersey,	https://www.state.nj.us/education/facilities/laws/act_summ.shtml
	New Mexico,	http://www.nmpsfa.org/legacy/redesign/pscoc.html
	Ohio,	http://ofcc.ohio.gov/
	West Virginia,	https://sba.wv.gov/Pages/default.aspx
	Wyoming,	http://sfd.wyo.gov/
	Washington, DC	https://dgs.dc.gov/page/dgs-healthy-schools
Stand-alone, State-assigned Board	Arkansas,	http://arkansasfacilities.arkansas.gov/facilities/construction
	California,	http://www.calschoolconstruction.dgs.ca.gov
	Maryland,	http://www.pscp.state.md.us/APG/FIN%20Original%20APG%20Revised%206-6-17.pdf
	New Hampshire,	https://www.education.nh.gov/program/school_approval/documents/ed321-2-2-17.pdf
	New Mexico	http://www.nmpsfa.org/legacy/redesign/pscoc.html
Advisory Committee	Colorado,	https://www.cde.state.co.us/cdefinance/capconstmain
	Massachusetts,	http://www.massschoolbuildings.org/
	New Mexico,	http://www.nmpsfa.org/legacy/redesign/pscoc.html
	South Carolina,	https://ed.sc.gov/districts-schools/school-planning-building/
	Washington	https://www.k12.wa.us/SchFacilities/Programs/SchoolConstructionProjects.aspx
Legislative Oversight	Arkansas,	http://arkansasfacilities.arkansas.gov/facilities/construction
	Connecticut,	http://portal.ct.gov/DAS/Office-of-School-Construction-Grants/ Office-of-School-Construction-Grants-Policies-and-Memos
	Minnesota,	https://education.mn.gov/MDE/dse/schfin/fac/cons/
	New Mexico,	http://www.nmpsfa.org/legacy/redesign/pscoc.html
	Wyoming	http://sfd.wyo.gov/

Notes: [a]Table 3.5 lists more than one agency for a jurisdiction because two or more agencies may assign funds and/or guide the construction process.

[b]The table does not list Idaho, Indiana, Iowa, Louisiana, Nebraska, Nevada, Oklahoma, South Dakota, and Wisconsin because these states did not allocate construction funds or offer guidance for districts.

funding before high-wealth districts. As such, equalized project (EP) funding resembles state aid formulas based on a district's fiscal capacity. EP grants are usually time-limited and building-specific commitments. The district in many instances must pass a local referendum to satisfy the local share before the state releases its portion (Wood et al., 2019).

For example, after the state legislature in Ohio appropriates capital dollars in the biennium budget, the OFCC, an independent commission established by the legislature, accepts the capital funding allocation for distribution. The OFCC specifically furnishes construction management services and project oversight to primary and secondary public school districts through the Classroom Facilities Assistance Project, the primary construction funding option (Ohio School Facilities Commission, 2019).

As an EP, this program ranks all Ohio's public school districts by each district's property wealth (i.e., assessed per-pupil property valuation). This wealth factor establishes priority for state assistance upon request; therefore, lower-wealth districts collect aid before high-wealth districts, after meeting application requirements. The wealth ranking also sets each district's local and state percentage shares. Other than the Classroom Facility Assistance Program, districts may apply for capital building funds through other programs—Alternative Facilities Assistance, Expedited Local Partnership, Exceptional Needs, or Vocational School Construction (Ohio School Facilities Commission, 2019).

Fifteen states (see table 3.6) approve state subsidies based on a project-based application (PBA) without regard to a district's wealth. Project-based programs resemble a flat grant, although the state's support rarely funds the full cost to construct a new building or renovate an existing structure. To evaluate and rank district applications, state agency staff members may consider submissions based on anticipated student enrollments, current building conditions, site locations, project justifications, planning documents, or local funding matches (Wood et al., 2019). Six states factor the disposable facility's age as a criterion to evaluate capital funding applications, although distribution methods vary (Brimley et al., 2020).

Pennsylvania's Department of Education implements a project-based program to distribute new construction and renovation reimbursement dollars for primary and secondary schools. With a distinct annual capital budget appropriation, the legislature earmarks the state's bond proceeds through the Commonwealth Financing Authority (PlanCon Advisory Committee, 2018).

To apply and secure reimbursement, a district staff must complete a Planning and Construction Workbook (PlanCon) to document the district's facility planning process, justify the project, assure state law and regulation compliances, and establish the financial commitment. The state education department's Division of School Facilities staff members review proposals by the plans for site acquisition, construction, competitive bids, and local funds; estimated student enrollments; and current building conditions (PlanCon Advisory Committee, 2018).

Based on the application criteria and available state subsidy, the department's Division of School Facilities staff ranks qualified plans, calculates the state share, and approves or denies the reimbursement. When a district is not interested in receiving a state reimbursement, project approval by the Division of School Facilities staff is unnecessary; however, districts must still follow applicable statutes to construct a public building, including American with Disabilities Act regulations, state competitive bid and prevailing wage laws, and building inspections along with fire code requirements (PlanCon Advisory Committee, 2018).

Eight states and the District of Columbia qualify construction, renovation, and building maintenance as a part of the district's total educational program. These states and the District of Columbia distribute capital categorical aid (CCA) with or without equalization principles (Wood et al., 2019).

For instance, to maintain, repair, or renovate facilities in Florida, capital revenue, assigned by the legislature, originates from state general obligation bonds, utility and communication services tax revenue, and/or motor vehicle license earnings. The legislature dedicates construction funds via CCA. The Florida Department of Education staff members distribute need-based capital outlay funds through the Public Education Capital Outlay and Debt Service Trust Fund based on each district's annual Five-Year District Facilities Work Plan that describes the age of district school buildings and facility square footage (Florida Department of Education, 2018).

The designated state education department staff tabulates new construction dollars in an equalized two-part formula with 40% distributed to districts based on the district's average student population over the past three years and 60% disbursed according to the district's average student attendance growth in the past three years (Florida Department of Education, 2018).

Six states allot capital funds through debt service programs. Two state programs equalize debt service (EDS) to judge district requests based on local property wealth. Two state programs do not employ a wealth factor; therefore, this fund distribution method evaluates requests on an unequal debt service (UDS) basis. Two state programs utilize both an equalized and unequalized basis to evaluate requests. Debt service programs represent categorical aid for a specific purpose (e.g., debt), with variations between project-based and loan programs (Wood et al., 2019).

A debt service program reimburses districts solely on the district's annual incurred bond indebtedness (i.e., principal and interest). This type of program does not consider the actual construction costs. Alaskan schools, for example, may receive 60% to 70% reimbursement for the principal and interest incurred by a district in a construction or renovation project (Wood et al., 2019).

Texas' equalized debt service program reimburses districts to repay debt on qualifying bonds with the state's share averaging 57% of the total district debt over the past three years. Districts may request assistance in each biennium budget, but the district must repay the settlement within eight years (Wood et al., 2019; Texas Education Agency, 2019a).

Kentucky's Facilities Support Program for capital construction represents an example of an equalized and unequalized debt service program. Kentucky voters must approve a local nickel tax (five mills) levy before state funding becomes available to a district. This nickel tax levy solely applies to real and personal property tax; thus, when applying for state monies, a district's bond indebtedness is unequal due to dissimilar assessed property valuations between districts (Kentucky Department of Education, 2019).

After passing the nickel tax levy, the state equalizes the aid by factoring 150% of the statewide average per-pupil assessed property valuation to the local assessment. To equalize a district's incurred debt and ascertain the state's contribution, five mills of the state's average per-pupil assessed property valuation minus the local nickel tax revenue equals the state funding (Kentucky Department of Education, 2019).

Five states employ a loan program (LP) for school capital outlay, although the Indiana legislature and governor have not recently allotted construction loan funds (Brimley et al., 2020). State loan programs grant indirect state aid to districts. North Dakota's Construction Loan Program, for instance, is quite simple. The district electorate must pass a bond referendum before beginning the loan process. After bond approval by the voters, the district may apply to the North Dakota Department of Public Instruction for a construction loan (North Dakota Legislative Council, 2019).

Upon receipt of a loan request, the department's designated staff members determine eligibility by comparing the district's assessed property valuation with the state's average assessed property valuation. After loan eligibility determination, the specific department staff submits a district priority list based on the ages of the potentially replaced or remodeled structures, students' academic needs, occupancies, building designs, local community assistances, and project costs (North Dakota Legislative Council, 2019).

The Bank of North Dakota, the only bank in the United States owned by the state, then accepts the department's priority list. Interested districts apply for and may be granted 70% to 90% of the project cost as a loan. After bank approval, the district begins construction and loan repayment (North Dakota Legislative Council, 2019).

Because statewide general obligation bonds back most state loan programs, the state's credit rating may be stronger than a district's rating. The state loan program with potentially lower borrowing rates, therefore, may be a more viable funding option than a school construction loan without the state program (Wood et al., 2019).

Five states deliver school construction support through a state bond guarantee (SBG) program (Wood et al., 2019). California's exclusive construction funding source, for instance, utilizes general obligation bonds that voters approve statewide. The state's credit rating secures the interest rate. Coordinated with the SBG program, the California legislature and governor apportion the bond allocation fund (AF) within the annual operating budget. The legislature appropriates these restricted monies for career-technical school infrastructure and public schools' new construction, modernization, and special circumstances, such as critically overcrowded buildings, high-performance incentives, and financial hardship (California Office of Public School Construction, 2019).

Upon an approved application, the assigned California Department of Education staff and personnel at the State Allocation Board prioritize the state's allocation, by project, based on the number of district pupils, grade levels, and classrooms. Eligible districts obtain a general obligation bond allocation (California Office of Public School Construction, 2019).

A number of states combine distribution approaches. Districts in Massachusetts allocate state construction funds via an application based on equalized elements with the SBG incorporated as an application criterion. Agency staffs in Ohio, Oregon, and West Virginia approve application requests among applying districts based on equalizing factors and other variables. Six states factor the age of the existing facility into the decision process (Filardo, 2016; Wood et al., 2019).

Thirteen states have not recently allocated state aid for public school construction or renovation (Filardo, 2016). Oklahoma has a building equalization program, but the state has never allocated any money for a public school capital construction project because an education association (i.e., union) lawsuit blocked funding. Indiana has a loan program, although the state has not distributed funds in years (Wood et al., 2019). Table 3.6 lists primary and secondary public schools' capital funding distribution methods by jurisdiction.

Besides construction, renovation, and debt service funding programs, states also finance targeted competitive or entitlement grants for capital outlay. States most commonly apportion school safety, security, and technology capital investments funds through specific onetime or recurrent grants (Cramer et al., 2017).

In the wake of school shootings, 10 states allotted school entitlement or competitive security grants on a need basis. Nine additional states recently passed or await pending legislation aimed at school security funding (Cramer et al., 2017). Allowable expenditures for these state grants may retrofit

Table 3.6 Public School Capital Funding Distribution Methods[a]

Jurisdiction	*EP*	*PBA*	*CCA*	*UDS*	*EDS*	*LP*	*SBG*	*AF*
Alabama			X					
Alaska				X				
Arizona			X					
Arkansas				X				
California							X	X
Colorado		X						
Connecticut	X							
Delaware	X							
Florida			X					
Georgia		X						
Hawaii		X						
Kansas	X							
Kentucky		X		X	X			
Maine		X						
Maryland	X	X					X	X
Massachusetts	X	X					X	
Minnesota		X	X			X		
Mississippi			X					
Montana	X							X
New Hampshire	X							
New Jersey	X				X			
New Mexico	X							
New York	X							X
North Carolina						X		
North Dakota						X		
Ohio	X	X						
Oregon	X	X						
Pennsylvania		X						
Rhode Island	X							
South Carolina		X						
Texas			X	X	X	X	X	
Utah			X				X	
Vermont		X						
Virginia			X			X		X
Washington	X							
Washington, DC			X					
West Virginia	X	X						
Wyoming		X						X
Total[b]	15	15	9	4	2	5	5	6

Notes: [a]The table does not list Idaho Illinois, Indiana, Iowa, Louisiana, Michigan, Missouri, Nebraska, Nevada, Oklahoma, South Dakota, Tennessee, and Wisconsin because these states have not granted any recent capital funding to school districts.

[b]The total for all categories does not equal 51 because a number of jurisdictions employ a variety of capital funding distribution and debt service methods.

Sources: Brimley et al. (2020), Filardo (2016), and Wood et al. (2019).

schools with bulletproof windows, panic buttons, or armored classrooms, although most grants allocate monies for resource officers' expenses and staff trainings (Reuters Staff, 2018).

Two times in past history, the federal government legislated support for primary and secondary public school infrastructure. The Emergency Relief Appropriation Act of 1935 (i.e., Works Progress Administration, 1935–1949) built schoolhouses, roads, bridges, and other public structures.

The American Recovery and Reinvestment Act (2009) authorized a one-time appropriation via the State Fiscal Stabilization Fund to stimulate job creation following the 2008 economic recession. Congress legislated dollars to invest in critical areas, such as energy, health care, and education. A portion of the allocated monies was for school modernization through bonds for renovation, maintenance, and construction. Other federal infrastructure initiatives were either short-lived or unfunded, such as the Education Infrastructure Act (1994) and the Consolidated Appropriations Act (2001) for school renovation and repair under Part B of the Individuals with Disabilities Education Act (Alexander & Alexander, 2019; Congressional Research Service, 2015).

The Federal Emergency Management Agency (FEMA), at present, administers a disaster assistance program (i.e., Public Assistance Grant Program) to meet the needs of students, schools, and states devastated by a natural catastrophe. School building modernization, renovation, repair, debris removal, and safety measures are allowable expenses with FEMA funding (Alexander & Alexander, 2019; Congressional Research Service, 2015).

Monies appropriated by the federal government from entitlements may allow expenditures for infrastructure and renovation. The Individuals with Disabilities Education Act (IDEA), for example, permits expenditures for assistive devices (e.g., wheelchairs and frequency modulation listening systems) and specialized computer hardware. By permission from the U.S. Secretary of Education, school districts may utilize IDEA funds for building modifications (e.g., elevator installation) to accommodate disabled students (Alexander & Alexander, 2019; Congressional Research Service, 2015).

Title I of the Elementary and Secondary Education Act (1990) allows expenditures to remodel "small spaces," rewire technology structures, and purchase technology hardware. A school administrator should review each federal entitlement's allowable expenses before purchasing equipment, retrofitting infrastructure, or starting a renovation project with these monies (Alexander & Alexander, 2019; Congressional Research Service, 2015).

Specific competitive federal grants may also finance capital expenses. The Secure our Schools Grant Program (https://www.k12grants.info/GrantDetails.aspx?gid=14769), for example, focuses on school security and safety measures. Surveillance cameras, security systems, door locking mechanisms, outdoor lighting, metal detectors, finger scanning identification devices, laptops and printers for security, fire extinguishers, school bus video cameras, rapid communication systems, two-way radios, and defibrillators were allowable expenses.

The Project School Emergency Response to Violence (https://www2.ed.gov/programs/dvppserv/index.html), another competitive needs-based program, assists local educational agencies with two grant opportunities (e.g., immediate and extended services) that support recovery from a violent/disruptive event or an undue financial hardship in response to a crisis. The Extended Services grant permits expenses related to minor repairs, temporary security measures, and portable devices (e.g., metal detectors and video cameras).

Corporate awards, foundation grants, and personal donations may fund public school building repairs, expansions, and other capital improvements. For example, the Metropolitan Regional Arts Council Capital Grant (https://mrac.org/grants/capital) provides up to $10,000 for nonprofit organizations in Minnesota to improve a building or purchase infrastructure (e.g., metal detectors and security cameras), although full-scale construction and permanent security measures are not funded.

The school board, superintendent, and CFO/treasurer are key participants in establishing cash reserves or sinking funds, electing to place a bond referendum on the ballot, and/or pursuing state or federal capital dollars. The building principal and other school administrators may access current building appropriations for minor capital projects to renovate or modernize buildings.

CAPITAL FUNDING FOR NONPUBLIC AND PUBLIC CHARTER SCHOOLS

Nonpublic Schools

Nonpublic schools have limited access to state and federal funds; therefore, school officials must investigate a variety of avenues to fund capital expenditures, such as personal pledges as well as corporation, foundation, and philanthropic grants. Cash donations, estate commitments, and planned gifts may impact capital funding for schools because planned gifts account for a large number of major capital campaign dollars (Worth, 2019).

A number of corporate, foundation, and philanthropic organizations deliver financial resources for school infrastructure and construction. Articles in *The Chronicle of Philanthropy* and information on the Philanthropy website (http://philanthropy.com) may assist school officials in becoming familiar with planned giving topics. To garner dollars for capital investments successfully, nonpublic school officials should execute a capital campaign (Worth, 2019).

A successful capital campaign consists of two phases: quiet and public (Worth, 2019). To review the phases, click or search for the Grantspace website at https://grantspace.org/resources/blog/capital-campaigns-the-quick-and-painless-beginner-s-guide/. NonProfitPro [https://www.nonprofitpro.com/webinars/] offers a plethora of resources and DonorSearch [https://www.donorsearch.net/education/] delivers capital campaign services for a fee.

Cash donations often derive from either a direct appeal or fundraiser. Estate commitments and planned giving, on the other hand, refer to a charitable gift that requires more donor forethought and planning to execute than a cash donation. Givers, by action, arrange planned gifts during their lifetime, but the will endowment, trust, charitable annuity, and transferred asset bequeath upon death. When identifying organizations for support, school officials, particularly at religious schools, should identify those givers with a mission and core values that align with the school's beliefs (Worth, 2019).

School leaders and capital campaign organizers should seek to collaborate with small business owners who hold strong community bonds and may be easier to contact for contributions than large corporate executives. Before contacting companies, promoters should consider the establishment's incentive to support the initiative. Preparing literature with key talking points facilitates the sales promotion (Worth, 2019).

Monetary gifts from businesses may not be the only form of giving for schools. Companies, in fact, also donate in-kind support, equipment, or staff time and expertise. School officials should not ignore building relationships with company employees who may personally choose to donate, even when the business does not contribute (Worth, 2019).

Public Charter Schools

Public charter schools mainly rely on state and federal funding to finance facility renovation and construction, although five states (Alaska, Colorado, Florida, New Mexico, and Ohio) permit charter schools to access local property tax for facilities. States offer financial facility assistance to public charter schools in various ways, including dedicated basic aid allocations, revenue bond plans, grants, public loans, and credit enhancement programs (Ziebarth, 2019).

Public charter schools in 17 states and the District of Columbia access per-pupil facility allowances via state aid. Arizona, California, Georgia, Minnesota, New York, and the District of Columbia provide more than $1,000 per pupil. Arkansas, Florida, Indiana, Massachusetts, and New Mexico grant between $351 and $999 per pupil, whereas Colorado, Idaho, Ohio, Pennsylvania, Tennessee, Texas, and Utah grant less than $350 per student (Ziebarth, 2019).

Public charter schools in 23 states may finance facilities with revenue bonds supported by state income. When a charter school fails to make a bond debt payment, the state can withhold a portion of the school's basic aid to cover the missed payment (Education Commission of the States, 2018a).

Fourteen states and the District of Columbia authorize facility grant programs for charter schools, although only eight jurisdictions (Arkansas, California, Connecticut, Georgia, New York, Ohio, Tennessee, and the District of Columbia) actually funded grants. Eleven states ensure that charter schools may access existing state grants and revenues (Ziebarth, 2019).

Although 13 states and the District of Columbia authorize public loans for public charter facilities, only nine jurisdictions (California, Colorado, Connecticut, Indiana, Nevada, South Carolina, Tennessee, Utah, and the District of Columbia) actually funded grants. Public charter schools in Indiana, for instance, may access low interest state loans, when legislatively allocated. Although the Louisiana legislature has never funded the charter school start-up loan program, charter law allows loans without interest up to $100,000 for three years (Ziebarth, 2019).

Eight states and the District of Columbia offer varying forms of credit enhancement programs. Seven states do not offer facility funding for public charter schools, and three states do not specifically apportion state construction funding for public charter schools (Education Commission of the States, 2018a). To see public charter school funding for capital projects in a specific state and the District of Columbia, click or search for the Education Commission of the States site at http://ecs.force.com/mbdata/mbquestNB2C?rep=CS1719 and the National Alliance for Public Charter Schools at https://www.publiccharters.org/our-work/charter-law-database/components/19.

Two distinct federal programs grant financial facility assistance to public charter schools. The State Charter School Facilities Incentive Grant Program (https://innovation.ed.gov/what-we-do/charter-schools/state-charter-school-facilities-incentive-grants/) stipulates competitive grants for states to establish or administer aid for charter school facilities. Federal funds from this grant match nonfederal dollars dedicated to charter schools. The federal share decreases each year from 90% to 20% over five years.

The Credit Enhancement for Charter School Facilities Program (https://innovation.ed.gov/what-we-do/charter-schools/credit-enhancement-for-charter-school-facilities-program/), designed to improve a charter school's credit standing, reduces the financial risk to creditors for private loans and revenue bonds. For the fiscal year 2020, the presidential request for charter schools at the time of publication was $500 million (U.S. Department of Education, 2019).

Similar to traditional public schools, monies appropriated by the federal government from entitlements may allow infrastructure and renovation expenditures at public charter schools. The Individuals with Disabilities Education Act (2015), for instance, permits expenses for the acquisition of assistive equipment and facility modifications. Title I funding, additionally, may purchase technology equipment, rewire technology, and remodel minor spaces at public charter schools (Congressional Research Service, 2015).

Corporations, foundations, and individual donations are potential private funding sources for public charter school infrastructures. Although a number of foundations assist with charter school facility funding within selected geographical markets, the two largest foundations with a wide geographical scope are the Bill and Melinda Gates Foundation (http://www.gatesfoundation.org) and the Walton Family Foundation (http://www.waltonfamilyfoundation.org/educationreform).

Besides foundation support for charter facilities, regional community development institutions and nonprofit financing organizations furnish charter school grants, construction and acquisition loans, bond support, and federal credit enhancements. For example, the Self-Help Venture Fund (https://www.self-help.org/who-we-are/self-help-family/self-help-ventures-fund) delivers loans. The Capital Impact Partners (https://www.capitalimpact.org/focus/education/) offers capital to finance the building and expansion of high-performing charter schools (Community Development Financial Institutions Coalition, 2019).

SUMMARY

To initiate a capital project, a district should develop a properly communicated and suitably crafted facility master plan in order to provide a backdrop for fruitful capital improvements. When considering a capital project, a district must explore funding options, including cash reserves; sinking fund accounts; bond sales; state and federal aid; or private, state, and federal entitlements as well as competitive grants.

With such dependence on local funding to build a new school or renovate an existing structure, a local bond referendum is the most common means. When a bond election is necessary, each jurisdiction's bond election law regulates procedures and passage rates. The local bonding process is very intricate and demands bond counsel services.

Jurisdiction funding is another frequently sought source for primary and secondary public school districts to build a new school or renovate an existing building, when the jurisdiction offers such a program. Jurisdiction departments of education and other organizations guide the application process, award monies, and oversee construction or renovation.

Federal funding for public and nonpublic school capital investments is rather limited, although funding is available for charter schools. Corporation, foundation, philanthropic organizations, and private donations pose other opportunities for capital campaign dollars at public, nonpublic, and charter schools.

A major capital project is a complex undertaking due to multiparty involvement; budgetary considerations; regulatory guidelines; and local, state, and federal statutory regulations. When necessary, the school board approves the facility master plan and bond referendum, accepts state funding, selects the bond counsel and architectural firm, approves budgets and appropriations, authorizes competitive bids and payment schedules, and oversees the entire process.

District administrators plan capital projects, secure local and jurisdiction funding, assist with bond counsel and architecture firm selection, manage budgets and appropriations; and supervise the process. Community, school board, and staff perceptions of a final construction project define project success. School leaders must be well versed in funding options and related processes to direct productive facility planning and secure capital investment funding.

PROJECTS

1. Survey stakeholders regarding the status of school/district capital assets and prioritize needs.
2. Research and report the capital funding means for your district to address needs—cash reserves; sinking funds; permanent improvement levies; bond issues; state, federal, and private grants; cash donations; and/or planned giving initiatives.
3. Conduct a review and report your jurisdiction's capital outlay information, including budget timeline, asset definitions, life spans, and approved expenditures (e.g., maintenance) by accessing the *Capital Budgeting in the States* full report at https://www.nasbo.org/mainsite/reports-data/capital-budgeting-in-the-states.
4. Report your jurisdiction's bond election laws by accessing the Ballotpedia website at https://ballotpedia.org/Voting_on_school_bond_and_tax_measures.
5. Examine and report the processes that your jurisdiction exercises to fund school construction and renovation.

6. Develop a preliminary capital budget for a building construction or renovation.
7. Participate in a capital campaign, permanent improvement levy as allowed by law, or bond issue election when permitted by your jurisdiction.
8. Apply for a capital project grant.
9. Participate in or lead a new construction or renovation.

Chapter 4

School Finance Challenges

OBJECTIVES

After reading this chapter, you should be able to

- ✓ investigate a jurisdiction's tax system and devise a sound tax policy (NELP 1.2, 3.2, 5.2, 5.3, 6.1, 6.2, 7.3, 7.4);
- ✓ identify and analyze escalating expenditures in a district/school appropriation and create a plan to address rising line-item costs (NELP 1.2, 6.1, 6.2, 7.3, 7.4);
- ✓ analyze a jurisdiction's budget and assess the funding distribution formula with regard to adequacy and equity provisions (NELP 1.2, 3.2, 4.1, 5.3, 6.1, 6.2);
- ✓ identify a district's unfunded plus underfunded mandates and examine the cost of each corresponding line-item appropriation (NELP 5.3, 6.1, 6.2, 7.3, 7.4); and
- ✓ describe adequacy cost study processes and justify potential programs/resources for a school to achieve student academic success (NELP 1.2, 3.2, 4.1, 5.3, 6.1, 6.2, 7.3).

Complex historical, political, and economic landscapes distinguish each state's tax structure that finance public services, including primary and secondary public education. With unique processes, each of the 50 states and the District of Columbia operate distinctive revenue means and public education funding distribution systems detailed in state laws and regulations (Odden & Picus, 2020).

Financing America's public schools predominantly derives from three sources—local, state, and federal. The larger funding portion between local and state sources depends upon community wealth and state equalization formulas. Because of interlinked local and state funding sources in addition to complicated variables in state basic aid formulas, school funding processes confuse most people; even school finance experts find primary and secondary public education funding a confusing maze (Odden & Picus, 2020).

Educational choice, particularly in the form of vouchers and publicly funded charter schools, further muddies the school finance narrative. Fair and comprehensible taxation principles, understandable and efficient delivery systems, as well as equitable and adequate funding levels for schools must align with today's needs (Barba, Ginn, Grusendorf, & Heflin, 2016; Brimley et al., 2020).

School finance policies and funding allocations are inherently political. Acknowledging the facts and dismissing deceptive proclamations to filter biases in school finance research becomes challenging. A number of pundits and politicians from both sides of the aisle, for instance, occasionally proclaim that money does not matter in delivering a quality primary and secondary education. This misleading opinion often migrates to unsupportable presumptions that funding cuts do not harm school processes, and schools can achieve favorable student academic results in spite of reductions (Baker, 2018; Baker, Di Carlo, & Weber, 2019).

To aggravate school finance research, Burnette II (2019) reported that state education departments do not have sufficient technology to track the federal, state, and local dollars for district officials and policymakers to make sound decisions. Unclear data, which is often two to three years old, frustrates both school funding advocates and conservative accountability hawks who claim reform efforts are impossible with indistinct primary and secondary education financial details. Nevertheless, researchers have told advocates as well as federal and state lawmakers that more specific, up-to-date spending data will show where states can make cost savings and districts need more money.

On the other hand, with detailed datasets and empirically grounded research to examine relationships between money and student outcomes, many school finance scholars dispute the assertion that funding does not matter. According to a number of researchers, increases in per-pupil revenue positively correlate to student academic gains; however, school leaders must wisely spend the public dollars (Baker, 2018; Gigliotti & Sorensen, 2018; Kreisman & Steinberg, 2019).

According to the Kreisman and Steinberg (2019) study, a $1,000 annual increase in foundation funding or a 10% increase in expenditures garnered a 0.1 standard deviation increase in reading scores and nearly a 0.08 standard deviation increase in math marks. In this study, dropout rates declined, and graduation rates marginally increased. The authors remarked that notable gains accrue for students in later grades with increased funding, particularly at poorer districts.

Gigliotti and Sorensen (2018) researched the variation in per-pupil expenditures from a specific provision of the state aid formula in New York State that permitted districts to maintain prior levels of total state aid, although a district's student enrollment declined. Gigliotti and Sorensen uncovered achievement gains of approximately 0.047 standard deviations in math and 0.042 standard deviations in English when applying an additional $1,000 in per-pupil spending.

Baker (2018) examined the advancements of students' academic outcomes in relationship to funding for added pupil support services, small class sizes, and competitive teacher compensation. According to a substantial body of literature, teachers' wages influenced student learning in two contexts: qualifications for those who choose to enter the profession and invested teacher time. In explanation, strong teacher credentials, therefore, usually equated to better student academic outcomes than achievement results from teachers with weak credentials, and inexperienced teachers often correlated to lower student educational performances than the learning effects from experienced teachers.

Studies that investigated the influences of alternative teacher compensation approaches (e.g., performance-based pay, signing bonuses, and salary differentials based on experience and training) reported neither a positive nor a negative relationship between teacher wages and students' learning (Baker, 2018). Overall, the empirical research in these sources strengthened the case that school resources and money matter, and sustained financial investments can improve students' academic performances.

Overwhelming research on the positive impact of early childhood education and prekindergarten programs supported investing public dollars in such programs to eliminate academic achievement gaps, particularly for diverse student groups (e.g., economically disadvantaged). Preschool programs also lessened nutrition and health issues for youngsters from poor and minority backgrounds and delivered constructive short- and long-term social as well as financial benefits for these youth (Sneha, García, Heckman, & Hojman, 2017; Weglarz-Ward, Ang, & Gaynes, 2019).

Weglarz-Ward et al. (2019) reported that funding streams along with state and federal policies in regard to early childhood education programs challenged services for preschool children with and without disabilities in Nevada's urban, rural, and tribal areas. Political action to change this phenomenon has been difficult.

While money alone may not solve public education students' scholastic issues, sustained positive progressions in funding levels with soundly devised distribution methods may lead to equitable, adequate school district allocations and high-performing student outcomes. Because state politicians hold the greatest control over school access to state primary and secondary public education dollars, state legislatures and governors influence public schooling outcomes for students.

Empirical literature validated that fruitful school finance reform in a number of states exhibited substantially positive effects on educational performance growth for all students, and the reforms diminished academic achievement gaps between diverse student groups. Research evidence revealed that appropriate levels of equitable and adequate per-pupil state funding combined with spending accountability epitomized promising phenomena to alleviate public education ills with regard to students' academic achievements (Baker, 2018).

Some politicians and reporters argued that charter schools achieved better educational results with less funding than traditional public schools. These proponents asserted that governing flexibility allowed charter schools to engage in more creative teacher compensation packages and implemented more productive teaching practices as well as superior learning methods than existed in conventional schools. Although some researchers credited student academic gains in charter schools with lower costs than traditional public schools, others characterized charter schools as a failed experiment that delivered significantly poorer student achievement results with similar or higher costs than traditional schools (Beck, Watson, & Maranto, 2019; Epple, Romano, & Zimmer, 2017).

García and Weiss (2019) asserted that some charter schools spend less money because they hired inexperienced staff and sustained high teacher turnover, while other charter schools expended more money and offered more competitive teacher wages and smaller class sizes than traditional public schools. According to Baker (2018), public charter schools, however, with varying funding means and instructional delivery methods, may unlock insights to leverage improved student learning resources than conventional schools.

After 50 years of debate on school finance policies, the following accords to advance student educational outcomes emerged from both academic literature and court rulings: money matters, resources matter, and equitable funding distribution methods with adequate funds count (Baker, 2018).

To unravel primary and secondary public funding challenges, consider the subsequent questions:

- Does the state tax system equitably raise revenue among low-, middle-, and high-income taxpayers along with corporations to finance public services (e.g., education) adequately?
- Is there an overreliance on property tax that affects equitable school funding?

- What local, state, and federal tax reforms will strengthen current taxation systems?
- What influence does state budget cuts have on students' educational achievements?
- Which escalating expenditures beyond the normal inflation rate confront school budgets and educational leaders?
- Do unfunded and underfunded mandates influence delivery of quality education services?
- Do states equitably distribute state and local public education dollars between diverse school districts (e.g., small, rural, intercity, and highly concentrated poverty)?
- Are state and local public education funds adequate to provide a quality standard education for all students?
- How has litigation and adequacy cost studies affected school finance reform initiatives?
- Where does nonpublic and charter school funding fit into the American school finance discussion?

In sum, policymakers should rely on first-rate research to guide critical decisions, including taxation and school finance reforms. School officials should judiciously spend accessible monies. Individuals interested in primary and secondary public education finance reforms must apply keen analytical skills to evaluate policies in relation to student learning outcomes.

AMERICAN TAX SYSTEM

Engraved on the exterior of the Internal Revenue Service federal headquarters in the District of Columbia is a quote from former U.S. Supreme Court justice Oliver Wendell Holmes: "Taxes are what we pay for a civilized society" (Avi-Yonah, 2006, p. 5). Governments depend on sustainable revenue for social programs; police, fire, and military protections; and public investments (e.g., schools, roads, libraries, and parks) in order to achieve goals for a prosperous, functional society; therefore, governments must collect taxes. No one relishes paying taxes; however, America's tax system remains the means by which citizens utilize public services that everyone expects and desires (Avi-Yonah, 2006).

Sound tax and fiscal governmental policies lead to economic growth and a suitable quality of life for all citizens. Over the years, tax policies and revenues raised by distinct governmental levels changed dramatically, with strategies overlapping between local, state, and federal governments (Goel, Saunoris, & Schneider, 2018).

To deliver public services efficiently, governments need a comprehensive tax system. Lawmakers at each governmental level should consciously promote regulations that institute just policies and fair individual as well as corporate tax collection processes.

Federal tax contributes the least to elementary and secondary public education funding; however, federal income tax accounts for the largest yield of all governmental revenue sources. With policy shifts over the years, the number of tax brackets, deduction and exemption levels, and tax-sheltered components changed numerous times. According to many authorities, federal income tax policy currently institutes a higher proportional rate for individuals, especially poorer taxpayers over corporations (Scheve & Stasavage, 2019).

When state lawmakers plan and evaluate state tax policy, policymakers must factor federal tax policies into the equation because federal income tax influences state income tax collection. To evaluate and analyze tax systems, economists and policymakers employ several metrics—base, rate, yield, fairness, stability, adequacy, elasticity, diversity, administrative efficiency, and taxpayer compliance (Brimley et al., 2020; Odden & Picus, 2020).

Taxes hold three fundamental features—base, rate, and yield. The tax base defines the object or source subject to tax (e.g., property, sales, and income). The rate applies a measurement unit to the tax base, such as a percentage or millage. Property, income, and sales tax demarcate broad-based taxes that assess large numbers of people (Brimley et al., 2020; Odden & Picus, 2020).

Yield describes the fully collected revenue by a tax source. Broad-based taxes produce high yields even with modest rates, whereas a narrow-based tax, such as a selective excise tax (e.g., tobacco and alcohol), yields limited revenue because fewer people contribute. A tax with high yields (e.g., property and income) is difficult to eliminate because such action necessitates huge cuts in governmental services or substantial increases in other taxing sources; neither outcome is commonly popular with the public (Brimley et al., 2020; Odden & Picus, 2020).

Taxpayers in a fair tax system contribute in proportion to their ability to pay. When taxpayers pay a fair proportion based on income, citizens more readily accept the tax and approve tax increases when necessary. When poor people pay proportionally more tax than wealthy individuals, tax analysts portrayed that structure as regressive, unfair, and inequitable (Scheve & Stasavage, 2019).

When lawmakers choose to support federal and state budgets with regressive taxes predominately collected from low- and middle-income taxpayers than high-income taxpayers, public support for the tax normally erodes, especially when the tax is subject to voter approval. To measure a tax system's equality, analysts study the fairness level of all taxing sources and the state's reliance on each tax. Most states rely on a combination of regressive and progressive taxes (Brimley et al., 2020).

Because taxes fund critical public services, tax authorities measure taxes to meet funding needs by the following measures—adequacy, reliability, stability, and elasticity. An adequate tax system raises sufficient revenue to sustain necessary services and produce notable outcomes. Sound tax systems exhibit reliability and stability during fiscal downturns or high unemployment. Stable, reliable taxes yield satisfactory revenue in the face of changing economic circumstances because these tax types grow at a predictable, steady pace to meet increasing demands (Brimley et al., 2020).

Elasticity measures a tax's yield responsiveness during economical changes. Elastic taxes (e.g., individual income tax) fluctuate over time as the state's economy expands or wanes. To some degree, stability and elasticity counterbalance each other because elastic tax yields tend to be less stable in a recession, whereas stable tax (e.g., property tax) yields are less elastic but steady during fiscal slumps (Odden & Picus, 2020).

To neutralize fiscal swings from a single tax, diversification with yields from two or more broad-based tax bases allows localities to capitalize on a mix of varying strengths and weaknesses in tax characteristics. For instance, individual and corporate income tax along with sales tax is inherently cyclical by economical terms, but property tax remains more stable. Inclusive tax yields that combine individual and corporate income, sales, and property taxes maintain a stable, yet elastic, revenue stream (Brimley et al., 2020).

An effectual tax system transparently administers tax law in a comprehensible manner with low administrative costs. Compliance for individuals and corporations must be straightforward, with understandable tax codes and fitting payment schedules. Confusing tax regulations breed discontent from individuals. An income tax system with loopholes, for example, grants those individuals who can afford well-informed accountants an advantage over individuals who digest tax codes and complete forms without expert support. Complex tax laws are difficult for governments to monitor and enforce (Wiehe et al., 2018).

State constitutions, statutes, and legal rulings clarify as well as guide decisions regarding tax collections and allocations. To fund public services, state and local governments historically finance public services on three broad-based taxes—individual income, property, and consumption (e.g., sales and excise). Narrow-based tax (e.g., estate, severance, and inheritance) yields and restrictive nontax revenue (e.g., intergovernmental transfers, insurance trusts, and other such state revenue) generally denote minimal income sources for public schools (Wiehe et al., 2018).

The following U.S. jurisdictions' average percentages of the total state tax collection in the 2018 fiscal year were property, 2%; sales, 46.7%; individual income, 42.7%; and the remaining taxes, 8.6% (U.S. Census Bureau, 2019b). (Note: This nationwide survey with the 2018 fiscal year data is the most current Census Bureau information for state revenue at the time of publication.) Table 4.1 details broad-based tax collection percentages by jurisdiction and source during the 2018 fiscal year.

Broad-based taxes, such as sales and individual income, are clearly affected by economic changes, while property tax, another broad-based tax, remains more stable than the others. According to Wiehe et al. (2018), consumers have fewer dollars during a fiscal downturn to purchase merchandise and generally resist spending; thus, sales tax yields decline.

To the contrary, when the economy expands, consumer purchases resulting in sales tax increases. Sales tax is less elastic than income tax but more susceptible to economic changes than property tax. Because retailers typically collect and consumers generally pay sales tax at the point of sale, administration is simple and transparent with consumer and retailer compliance quite high. According to most tax analysts, sales tax is slightly regressive, although most states exempt certain purchases like food and prescription drugs. In general, low-income people spend a higher proportion of their earned income on sales tax than high-income individuals spend (Odden & Picus, 2020).

Local sales tax, permitted as a local income source for independent and dependent districts in Alaska, California, Georgia, Illinois, Louisiana, Nevada, New York, North Carolina, Vermont, and Virginia, maintains the same attributes as state sales tax (Wiehe et al., 2018).

According to tax analysts, narrow-based excise tax on specific products (e.g., severance, motor fuel, alcohol, and tobacco) is highly regressive and very slow to increase in yield over time. As a result, excise tax remains an inappropriate or inadequate school revenue source because this volatile tax is unstable due to collection variations from year to year (Brimley et al., 2020).

Excise tax on motor fuel, alcohol, and tobacco, however, is easy to administer and simple to collect at the point of sale. Low-income individuals pay a higher proportion of their income on motor fuel, alcohol, and tobacco tax than middle- and upper-income taxpayers pay (Chaloupka, Powell, & Warner, 2019). Legislators generally earmark motor fuel tax for highway maintenance, repair, and construction, but the tax fails to keep pace with inflation and typical economic growth.

Property tax stands as a stable tax that produces a reliable revenue stream because assessed values normally remain constant in economic downturns. Because property tax is less responsive (i.e., elastic) to economic growth than income tax, revenue rises more slowly, even when property valuation increases. School districts, therefore, must request voter approval with excess levies or budget consent to meet increased costs (Odden & Picus, 2020).

Property tax compliance remains rather straightforward with basic taxpayer understanding and mortgage escrow payments for many property owners. The property assessment process, however, burdens local authorities

Table 4.1 Jurisdiction Tax Collection Percentages, FY 2018[a]

Jurisdiction	*Property*	*General Sales*	*Individual Income*	*Other Taxes*	*Jurisdiction*	*Property*	*General Sales*	*Individual Income*	*Other Taxes*
Alabama	3.7%	50.0%	40.6%	5.7%	Nebraska	0	46.3%	49.6%	4.1%
Alaska	7.4%	15.4%[b]	12%[c]	65.2%	Nevada	3.5%	80%	0[c]	16.5%
Arizona	6.4%	59.6%	30.2%	3.8%	New Hampshire	14.0%	35.1%[b]	30.1%[d]	20.8%
Arkansas	12.3%	49.1%	33.1%	4.8%	New Jersey	0	43.6%	48.8%	7.6%
California	1.6%	30.7%	61.5%	6.2%	New Mexico	1.5%	50.9%	23.7%	23.9%
Colorado	0	38.6%	55.2%	6.2%	New York	0	29.8%	63.7%	6.5%
Connecticut	0	40.3%	55.1%	4.6%	North Carolina	0	43.8%	47.9%	8.3%
Delaware	0	13.8%[b]	45.2%	41%	North Dakota	0.001%	33.2%	11.3%	55.5%
Florida	0	83.7%	5.2%[c]	11.1%	Ohio	0	62.1%	29.9%	20.2%
Georgia	3.9%	38.7%	53.6%	3.8%	Oklahoma	0	42.5%	39.0%	18.5%
Hawaii	0	61.3%	33.4%	5.3%	Oregon	0.002%	13.1%[b]	76.6%	10.3%
Idaho	0	49.4%	42.8%	7.8%	Pennsylvania	0	51.7%	37.6%	10.7%
Illinois	0.002%	46.9%	44.9%	8.2%	Rhode Island	0	48.3%	41.6%	10.1%
Indiana	0.001%	62.5%	33.6%	4%	South Carolina	0.004%	46.9%	46.0%	7.1%
Iowa	0.002%	46.5%	43.0%	10.5%	South Dakota	0	82.7%	1.7%[c]	15.6%
Kansas	7.5%	47.1%	40.3%	5.1%	Tennessee	0	72.5%	13.3%[d]	14.2%
Kentucky	5.5%	47.4%	41.5%	5.6%	Texas	0	85.3%	0[c]	14.7%
Louisiana	0.005%	60.4%	31.8%	7.8%	Utah	0	40.7%	54.6%	4.7%
Maine	1%	51.0%	40.6%	7.4%	Vermont	32.5%	33.4%	28.3%	5.8%
Maryland	3.6%	42.7%	47.0%	6.7%	Virginia	0.001%	30.2%	63.7%	6.1%
Massachusetts	0	30.4%	63.0%	6.6%	Washington	10.4%	76.5%	0[c]	13.1%
Michigan	7.0%	48.2%	37.2%	7.6%	Washington, DC	32.9%	24.2%	33.2%	9.7%
Minnesota	3.1%	39.8%	49.6%	7.5%	West Virginia	0.001%	50.4%	38.0%	11.6%
Mississippi	0.004%	63.8%	29.0%	7.2%	Wisconsin	1%	43.9%	48.3%	6.8%
Missouri	0.003%	42.5%	52.5%	5%	Wyoming	13.6%	47.0%	0[c]	39.4%
Montana	10%	21.5%[b]	50.2%	18.3%	Average	1.9%	46.8%	42.7%	8.6%

Notes: [a]The table, which includes the most current U.S. Census Bureau data at the time of publication, shows state-administered property tax percentages.

[b]Alaska, Delaware, Montana, New Hampshire, and Oregon do not collect a general state sales tax, although excise taxes were included as sales tax in the report.

[c]Alaska, Florida, Nevada, South Dakota, Texas, Washington, and Wyoming do not levy a state individual income tax, although a corporate income tax was included as income tax in the report.

[d]New Hampshire and Tennessee tax interest and dividend income only, although Tennessee phases out the interest and dividend income tax in 2021.

Source: U.S. Census Bureau (2019b).

and taxpayers due to technical drawbacks and political complications. Many tax analysts classified property tax as regressive, even though a number of states enacted homestead exemptions, circuit breakers, and tax abatements that intended to reduce the property tax load on specific taxpayers (Odden & Picus, 2020).

Property tax across a state can create public education funding disparities between property-poor and property-rich districts because schools in wealthy communities have a greater fiscal capacity to raise local property tax yields than poor communities. As a result, property-rich districts typically can offer additional educational resources than schools in property-poor districts (Lueken & Shuls, 2019).

Because property wealth in many states varies widely from district to district, a number of state supreme court rulings found the state funding system in violation of constitutional equity requirements. State courts in these instances mandated school finance reform, which ordered a revised fund distribution formula to neutralize the property tax effect on school district revenue (Alexander & Alexander, 2019; Baker, Farrie, & Sciarra, 2018).

Traditionally, state income tax maintains stable and elastic taxing properties. Although many state legislatures modified rates over the years, state individual income tax revenue across the nation generally has not significantly declined in times of economic downturns with the exception of the 2008 recession and shortly thereafter (Odden & Picus, 2020).

As individual income increases, in general, this tax yield correspondingly rises. State income tax typically remains progressive, and this broad-based tax exemplifies the fairest state revenue source. Well-devised standard deductions and exemption limitations strengthen fairness. Earned income credits also alleviate low-income taxpayers' tax burdens. With these adjustments and graduated tax rates, individual income tax sustains neutral economic effects that counterbalance regressive taxes (Odden & Picus, 2020).

Most state income tax systems closely mirror the federal income tax code, which is costly to administer and complex for most individuals and small business owners to understand. When connected to the federal structure, state individual income tax gains in efficiency and administration because taxpayers already maintain income records and calculate federal tax obligations. Taxpayer compliance is simple due to straightforward deductions from an individual's paycheck (Sjoquist, 2019). Local income tax for schools, permitted in Iowa, Kentucky, Ohio, and Pennsylvania, maintains the same basic characteristics as state and federal income tax.

Corporate income tax remains rather complex to comprehend, especially when a firm operates in more than one state, unless the company employs astute tax accountants and attorneys. This tax remains a minor percentage of state revenue due to tax incentives, aggressive tax planning, and the reclassification of business income to a passive investment (Sjoquist, 2019).

A just individual income tax and an inclusive corporate tax with reasonable graduated rates and minimal tax loopholes endure as cornerstones for a fair state tax system (Wiehe et al., 2018). Because states are highly dependent on elastic income and sales tax, revenues fluctuate when the economy weakens. During the 2008 recession and shortly thereafter, many states increased tax rates and cut budgets, although most states have rebounded economically at this time (Sjoquist, 2019).

Narrow-based tax revenue touches specific individuals, meaning that people pay estate and/or inheritance tax on the transfer of accumulated wealth at death or in anticipation of death. The yield from these taxes often fluctuates for states because forecasting remains a challenge.

Estate and/or inheritance taxes usually represent a small percentage of the overall state tax collection and expose the state to minimal fiscal risks, although income is rather unstable. Inheritance tax is typically collected from anyone who receives an inheritance and resides in one of the six states (Iowa, Kentucky, Maryland, Nebraska, New Jersey, and Pennsylvania) that impose an inheritance tax (Bell & Orem, 2019).

Twelve states (Connecticut, Hawaii, Illinois, Maine, Maryland, Massachusetts, Minnesota, New York, Oregon, Rhode Island, Vermont, and Washington) and the District of Columbia collect an estate tax. An estate tax is a tax on the transfer of property after death (Bell & Orem, 2019).

Estate tax equity is subject to considerable debate with proponents stating that these taxes prevent wealth accumulation and concentrated prosperity; opponents, to the contrary, claim death taxes are unfair because they may prevent family members from inheriting wealth from long-time investments, farms, or small businesses. Because probate courts commonly dispose of personal assets upon death, the state assumes the administrative burden, even though individuals must report asset transfers or arrange a means to forgo probate court resolutions. Many tax analysts contended that these taxes cause significant taxpayer compliance costs, particularly in estate planning (Munro & Murphy, 2019).

Nontax state revenue pertains to revenue from sources other than broad-based or narrow-based taxes. Intergovernmental transfer and insurance trust revenue stand as major collections for a state's nontax revenue. Intergovernmental transfer (e.g., Medicaid) funds entail money from federal subsidies to state governments. Insurance trust revenue derives from state pension collections, insurance program (i.e., workers' compensation) contributions, and net earnings on government investments. States also receive investment income from governmental obligation bonds backed by general revenue funds (Economic and Demographic Research, 2019; U.S. Census Bureau, 2019b).

Nontax revenue also generates from state-owned water, gas, and electric utility companies; liquor stores; and transits' service charges. Revenue related to alcohol in 17 monopoly states (Alabama, Idaho, Iowa, Maine, Michigan, Mississippi, Montana, New Hampshire, North Carolina, Ohio, Oregon, Pennsylvania, Utah, Vermont, Virginia, West Virginia, and Wyoming) and jurisdictions in Alaska, Maryland, Minnesota, and South Dakota stemmed from state-owned liquor store profits (Dadayan & Auxier, 2019).

State alcohol monopolies generated two to three times more revenue than states with a private license system. Monopoly states often earmark revenues from alcohol sales and licenses for specific uses, such as law enforcement or substance abuse treatment programs. Otherwise, these funds become unrestricted general fund income for state or local jurisdictions (Dadayan & Auxier, 2019).

State property sales and rentals, fines, and user fees typified other forms of nontax revenue (Economic and Demographic Research, 2019). In some instances, elected officials facing the dual reluctance to raise taxes and cut spending often approve increasing user fees, fines, or surcharges to fill budget gaps.

Restricted user fees for hunting or driver license charges typically finance licensing costs and related programs, although some states divert the income into the general fund. User fees are voluntary because the assessed person participates in the activity. Fines, often dedicated for specific purposes, are generally a function of the judicial proceedings with resultant revenue a secondary consideration (Economic and Demographic Research, 2019).

Gambling and lottery revenues constitute another nontax state revenue. These nontax revenues are regressive because poor individuals usually spend a higher proportion of their earned income on betting and sweepstakes than what wealthy individuals spend. Lottery and most gambling proceeds are unstable state revenue sources because income generated from associated activities often weakens after the introductory launch. Lottery and gambling provisions are expensive to manage with high oversight expenses (i.e., commission) and winner payouts (Economic and Demographic Research, 2019).

With forms of betting currently sanctioned by the government in all states except Utah and Hawaii, gambling advocates acknowledge that other states' residents pay a portion of these voluntary charges. Duties paid by nonresidents on gambling activities to augment state revenue appear especially palatable to some lawmakers who remain reluctant to increase broad-based tax rates (American Gaming Association, 2019).

Opponents of legalized gambling usually object to this nonrevenue source due to the morality of such tax. Legislators, on occasion, allot gambling revenues for specific purposes, which occasionally include primary and secondary public education. Lawmakers, in some cases, promise to increase state education spending with gambling revenue, when the initiative passes.

Legislators sometimes shift this income from dedicated public education allocations into the general fund, after initial voter approval. With this action, the total education budget remains the same, while districts lose the gambling or lottery proceeds from the initially approved intent.

With public services depending on state revenue collections, many tax analysts object to reliance on narrow-based taxes to fund public services. Legislators, however, may fear the political repercussions of enacting tax increases on more visible, broad-based taxes. Legislators, therefore, may view raises in narrow-based taxes as a safer political decision than increases in broad-based taxes (Metzer, Savoy, & Yayboke, 2019).

When public service costs surge, state legislators constantly probe to collect additional revenue from existing means and/or cultivate new tax bases. The South Dakota legislature in 2016, for example, passed a tax law that imposed sales tax obligations on out-of-state Internet retailers regardless of the corporate office location. The U.S. Supreme Court upheld the South Dakota law, with qualifications, to collect the remote sales tax in the landmark *South Dakota v. Wayfair* (2018) case. Supreme Court modifications established explicit definitions, an aggregate Internet sales minimum, simplistic taxation processes, and a ban on retroactive collections (National Conference of State Legislatures, 2019a).

Following the U.S. Supreme Court's decision, 37 states and the District of Columbia currently require remote sales tax collection. States that legislated post-*Wayfair* action primarily modeled their laws after the Supreme Court regulations. Missouri, Kansas, Tennessee, Florida, Louisiana, Oklahoma, Texas, and Arizona did not permit remote sales tax collection at the time of publication. Alaska, Delaware, Montana, New Hampshire, and Oregon did not collect sales tax. States that enacted tax changes requiring collection on remote sales estimated remote sales tax revenue ranging from $7 million to $190 million for fiscal year 2019 (National Conference of State Legislatures, 2019a).

Marijuana legalization generates another potential taxing source. Thirty-three states and the District of Columbia legalized marijuana for medical purposes. Alabama, Georgia, Idaho, Indiana, Iowa, Kansas, Kentucky, Mississippi, Nebraska, North Carolina, South Carolina, South Dakota, Tennessee, Texas, Virginia, Wisconsin, and Wyoming have not passed laws that legalize cannabis (i.e., marijuana) for medical or recreational purposes, although a number of states plan to pass legislation to legalize cannabis for medical purposes in the near future (National Conference of State Legislatures, 2019b).

Cannabis sales and/or excise tax imposed on retail transactions and distributor licensing fees may generate state revenue too (National Conference of State Legislatures, 2019b).

The revenue from taxable excise tax on legalized recreational cannabis for Colorado and Washington was $54.6 million in 2014, which was the first lawful year. Estimated combined state and local excise tax revenues for recreational cannabis in the six states with available data will surpass $1 billion annually in 2018. This income did not include revenue from gross receipts and individual income taxes nor license fees (Davis, Hill, & Phillips, 2019).

According to the Tax Inequality Index (Wiehe et al., 2018), most jurisdiction's tax systems were fundamentally inequitable because low- and middle-income taxpayers commonly shoulder a much higher ratio of tax burden than upper-income taxpayers bear. The Tax Inequality Index (Wiehe et al., 2018) measured each jurisdiction taxation system's effect on taxpayer incomes by comparing taxpayers' after-tax earnings by income groups (i.e., low, middle, and high).

To compare taxpayers' after-tax earnings by income groups, the tax inequality formula added the averages of three parts. Part 1 compared the richest 1% of taxpayers' average after-tax income in a jurisdiction with the poorest 20% of taxpayers' average after-tax income in a jurisdiction. Part 2 compared the richest 1% of taxpayers' average after-tax income in a jurisdiction with the middle 60% of taxpayers' average after-tax income in a jurisdiction (Wiehe et al., 2018).

Part 3 compared a half-weighted component—the top 20% of taxpayers' average after-tax income in a jurisdiction with the poorest 40% of taxpayers' average after-tax income in a jurisdiction. The sum of each part compared low-income taxpayers' after-tax incomes with high-income taxpayers' after-tax income in a jurisdiction, yielding the tax inequality percentage (Wiehe et al., 2018).

According to the above calculations on the Tax Inequality Index, the tax inequality percentage was regressive (i.e., negative percentages) in 45 jurisdictions, which meant low-income taxpayers' average after-tax incomes in the jurisdiction were proportionally less than high-income taxpayers' average after-tax incomes in the jurisdiction.

According to the Tax Inequality Index, Florida, Illinois, Nevada, Oklahoma, Pennsylvania, South Dakota, Tennessee, Texas, Washington, and Wyoming, the ten most regressive taxing jurisdictions, assessed low-income taxpayers at the bottom 20% of the income scale up to six times more than high-income taxpayers' duties. Middle-income taxpayers in these jurisdictions paid up to four times more tax than the high-income taxpayers paid. Both the absence of a graduated individual income tax scale and an overreliance on consumption taxes (e.g., sales and excise tax) contributed to these tax inequities (Wiehe et al., 2018).

Wiehe et al. (2018) further stated that the common tax system characteristics in these most regressive taxing jurisdictions were the following:

- Florida, South Dakota, Nevada, Tennessee, Texas, Washington, and Wyoming did not levy a broad-based individual income tax. According to Loughead and Wei (2019), Tennessee levied an individual income tax that only applied to interest and dividend income, although this tax will be eliminated in 2021.
- Although Pennsylvania, Illinois, and Oklahoma did levy an individual income tax, the graduated individual income tax rate scales in these states possessed fewer graduated income rates than those scales in less regressive jurisdictions. Pennsylvania and Illinois, for example, employed a flat tax rate; therefore, this system taxed high-income taxpayers' incomes the same rate as low-income taxpayers. Oklahoma, on the other hand, maintained a graduated rate structure, but the top taxable income tax rate started at $12,200 for married couples; thus, this taxing structure virtually taxed most taxpayers the same rate.
- Seven of the ten regressive jurisdictions relied heavily on regressive sales tax by collecting over three-fourths of their entire tax revenue from regressive taxes. According to the U.S. Census Bureau (2019b) for the 2018 fiscal year, Florida collected 83.7% of the total tax collection from sales and gross receipts taxes; Nevada, 80%; Oklahoma, 82.6%; South Dakota, 82.6%; Tennessee, 72.5%; Texas, 85.3%; and Washington, 76.5%.

California, Delaware, Minnesota, New Jersey, Vermont, and the District of Columbia illustrated the least regressive tax systems in the nation because these jurisdictions recorded positive percentages on the Tax Inequality Index, which meant low-income taxpayers' average after-tax incomes in the jurisdiction were slightly lower in proportion to high-income taxpayers' average after-tax incomes in the jurisdiction (Wiehe et al., 2018).

The common tax characteristics in the Wiehe et al. (2018) study for the more equitable tax systems were as follows:

- Each of these jurisdictions adopted a highly progressive individual income tax system with numerous graduated tax brackets and rates. California's tax system, for example, assigned 10 graduated income tax rate brackets and taxed individuals with income earnings over $1 million an additional assessment.
- Each jurisdiction in this group instituted an individual income tax system with few itemized deductions and restricted exemptions for high-income individuals. California, for instance, greatly limited tax breaks for upper-income taxpayers.
- Each of these jurisdictions offered refundable earned income tax credits that exceeded the federal individual income tax earned credit.
- Most jurisdiction's overall taxing system relied on progressive individual income tax revenue more than regressive sales and excise tax income.

According to the Wiehe et al. (2018) study, the nationwide average local and state (i.e., jurisdiction) tax rate in fiscal year 2015 (current data at the time of the study) for low-income taxpayers was 11.4% of their total income; the tax rate for middle-income taxpayers was 9.9% of their entire income; the tax rate for the top 1% of taxpayers was 7.4% of their full income.

Across the country, this discrepancy means that low-income American taxpayers paid as much as 1.5 times more of their earnings in taxes than the top 1% of taxpayers paid. Table 4.2 shows tax inequality ranks and percentages by jurisdiction.

Sound tax policies build strong economies and benefit public services, including education. When jurisdictions invest in first-class education systems through fair taxation, targeted investments promote greater equality and produce improved educational outcomes. In addition, infrastructure spending (e.g., school buildings, roads, bridges, public transit, and other physical

Table 4.2 Tax Inequality Rank and Percentage

Jurisdiction	*Inequality Rank*	*Inequality Percentage*	*Jurisdiction*	*Inequality Rank*	*Inequality Percentage*
Alabama	18	–4.6%	Nebraska	36	–2.0%
Alaska	26	–3.7%	Nevada	5	–7.1%
Arizona	11	–5.7%	New Hampshire	16	–5.0%
Arkansas	20	–4.2%	New Jersey	46	+0.6%
California	51	+2.5%	New Mexico	19	–4.5%
Colorado	35	–2.4%	New York	44	–0.5%
Connecticut	29	–3.2%	North Carolina	31	–3.0%
Delaware	48	+1.0%	North Dakota	17	–4.9%
Florida	3	–8.6%	Ohio	13	–5.1%
Georgia	27	–3.2%	Oklahoma	9	5.9%
Hawaii	15	–5.1%	Oregon	41	–1.2%
Idaho	38	–1.7%	Pennsylvania	7	–6.7%
Illinois[a]	8	–6.2%	Rhode Island	32	–2.8%
Indiana	12	–5.3%	South Carolina	39	–1.4%
Iowa[a]	21	–3.8%	South Dakota	4	–7.8%
Kansas	23	–3.6%	Tennessee	6	–6.9%
Kentucky	25	–3.2%	Texas	2	–8.8%
Louisiana	14	–5.1%	Utah	40	–1.2%
Maine	45	–1.9%	Vermont	49	+1.5%
Maryland	42	–0.2%	Virginia	33	–2.5%
Massachusetts	30	–3.1%	Washington	1	–12.5%
Michigan	22	–3.7%	Washington, DC	50	+1.5%
Minnesota	47	+0.9%	West Virginia	37	–1.7%
Mississippi	24	–3.5%	Wisconsin	33	–2.5%
Missouri	28	–3.2%	Wyoming	14	–6.1%
Montana	43	–0.7%			

Source: Wiehe et al. (2018).

assets) greatly supports the economy. Neglectful school facilities hurt students' health and academic performances, and by extension, long-term prosperity in the state and country suffers (Williams, 2017).

Gould (2015) reported federal tax reform failures from the past half century and described the lone success in 1986 by saying, "Tax reform may glide out of policymakers' mouths as an easy remedy for the country's ills; however, broad tax reform in fact requires a level of legislative skill, commitment, and cooperation far beyond what is usually available" (pg. 990).

Gould (2015) further defined a bipartisan political agenda for successful tax reform that eliminated logrolling (i.e., protecting political interests), disregarded lobbyists' influences, and established harmonious practices. To further explain these acts to build consensus, he proposed that the legislature should

- launch a fully bipartisan commitment with an endorsement from members of each political party at the outset,
- craft the tax reform law with transparency drafted by an unstoppable coalition,
- streamline and fast track debate procedures to curb negative disruptions and win support from rank-and-file members,
- employ staffs to test strategically controversial proposals, and
- maintain a "war room" mentality throughout the process to destroy disruptions.

Alongside this prescription for successful tax reform, state lawmakers should additionally execute the following actions to generate a tax reform consensus and craft an equitable, just state tax system, according to the Federation of Tax Administrators (2017) and Williams (2017):

- evaluate, adjust, and revise property tax structures by using well-trained assessors to deliver frequent, accurate assessments;
- pass well-designed graduated homestead exemption levels and circuit breaker rates adjusted for inflation to preserve reduction values for low-income taxpayers;
- incorporate fair property tax abatement regulations for property owners, corporations, and school districts;
- analyze state income tax fairness, modify rates by adding graduated tax brackets, and assign proportionally appropriate rates on corporations and the highest income taxpayers;
- revise state income tax credits by either adding earned credits to the structure when not available or changing current earned credits with low-income deduction caps and exemptions adjusted for inflation;

- eliminate state income tax loopholes that benefit only high-income taxpayers;
- tax corporate income with an appropriate franchise or gross receipts tax that combines company divisions' tax reporting to abolish shifting income tactics;
- enact corporate tax rules that command taxation where the sales originate to eliminate untaxed out-of-state retail sales;
- institute full disclosure laws that mandate a company to divulge actual profits and reveal paid taxes, tax credits, and abatements;
- examine and modernize the sales tax structure to contain a comprehensive set of untaxed services (e.g., personal, professional, and repairs) and Internet transactions;
- eliminate proportionally uneven, inefficient, and overly complex sales tax exemptions that offer tax relief for the wealthy; and
- launch mechanisms to monitor tax structures more quickly and deliver mid-year adjustments when necessary.

To remain vigilant for a just, effectual tax policy in support of public services, school officials should

- be well informed about the issues surrounding local, state, and federal tax systems;
- be precise about present tax system issues and those tax matters that impact school funding;
- engage lawmakers and the public in conversations about fair and equitable local, state, and federal tax policies;
- hold lawmakers accountable for just, equitable, and sustainable tax policies;
- rcspond appropriately to misleading or inaccurate statements about tax policies;
- react specifically about tax policies in relationship to school funding; and
- advocate strongly for tax reform that more evenly taxes all individuals and corporations to better serve the public.

BUDGET CUTS

Jurisdiction's financial investment in primary and secondary public schooling declined over the past decade primarily due to the 2008 recession that resulted in weakening sales tax growth and declining income tax receipts. Although total state tax revenue recovered nearly six years ago from its losses in the downturn, many states are still dealing with fallout over a decade after the 2008 recession. Policymakers in many states felt pressure to replenish rainy day funds for the next inevitable downturn, fund higher state employees' healthcare costs, and deal with unfunded pension liabilities rather than replenish primary and secondary education funding (The Pew Charitable Trusts, 2019b).

According to The Pew Charitable Trusts (2019b), primary and secondary state public education funding remains below the prerecession level in 29 states. Arizona's 2016 primary and secondary education budget was 24% below the prerecession budget, and 10 states remained over 10% below the 2008 amount. Ten states increased primary and secondary budgets between 0% and 5% over the 2008 point; four states, 6% to 10%; and seven states, over 11%. Between 2008 and 2016, North Dakota doubled the primary and secondary public education budget, which greatly exceeded the increase in other states. The District of Columbia did not submit funding data.

Because many schools rely on basic state aid, restoring state educational funding to prerecession levels remains an urgent priority because budget cuts cause school districts to reduce staff and delay educational reform efforts. Deep state reductions, therefore, force school districts to increase local funds to cover the shortage, scale back educational services, or implement a combination of both alternatives (The Pew Charitable Trusts, 2019b).

Local funding for schools, particularly property tax yields, also slowed after the 2008 recession, aggravating state reductions. Because property tax is more stable than sales and income tax, this local revenue source typically averages a 1.7% growth, but this meager increase did not fully compensate districts for the state and federal reductions.

Declining federal education dollars affect specific entitlement programs. Total spending by the U.S. government for primary and secondary education decreased from $58.3 billion in 2016 to $55.3 billion in 2017, representing a 5.2% reduction (U.S. Census Bureau, 2019a). The 2018 appropriation recorded another 1% reduction to $55 billion, and the 2019 appropriation remained the same as 2018 (U.S. Department of Education, 2019).

Although the president's fiscal year 2020 budget recommendation to U.S. Congress proposed eliminating funding for Title II, Title IV, and Title VI, Part A, Subpart 1 along with 26 other programs, all programs were reinstituted in the final adopted budget bill (House Committee on Appropriations, 2019; U.S. Department of Education, 2019). According to the National Education Association (2019), Every Student Succeeds Act fiscal year 2020 funding increased 7.1% over the fiscal year 2019 appropriation.

Reductions in funding undermine schools' capacities to develop the next generation's academic abilities and implement school initiatives, such as small teacher-to-student ratios and early childhood education programs. The future of the country depends on well-educated children. Because school funding intertwines between local, state (i.e., jurisdiction), and federal sources, examining each sources' funding trends stands important to grasp future public education revenue.

Table 4.3 ranks states according to the average state and local revenues for primary and secondary public school districts with percentage changes for

Table 4.3 State and Local Per-Pupil Revenue Rankings and Percentage Changes (2008–2016)

Jurisdiction	*State Revenue Rank*	*Rank and Percentage Change*	*Local Revenue Rank*	*Combined Rank and Percentage Change*	*Jurisdiction*	*State Revenue Rank*	*Rank and Percentage Change*	*Local Revenue Rank*	*Combined Rank and Percentage Change*
Alabama	34	3 (−21.6%)	41	7 (−15.4%)	Nebraska	46	36 (+3.1%)	12	43 (+6/4%)
Alaska	2	46 (+27.6%)	31	49 (+22/1%)	Nevada	27	20 (−7.9%)	45	4 (−18.6%)
Arizona	49	1 (−36%)	34	2 (−24.6%)	New Hampshire	35	23 (−3.6%)	7	45 (+11%)
Arkansas	11	33 (+ 2%)	49	31 (+0.3%)	New Jersey	10	26 (−2.7%)	4	28 (−0.9%)
California	22	14 (−11.8%)	33	14 (−5.8%)	New Mexico	13	16 (−11.7%)	47	11 (−8.3%)
Colorado	38	37 (+3.4%)	22	21 (−4%)	New York	5	25 (−2.8%)	2	44 (+9.8%)
Connecticut	9	45 (+16.3%)	3	46 (+11.7%)	North Carolina	32	12 (−12.2%)	46	3 (−19.6%
Delaware	7	17 (−10.0%)	18	23 (−2.6%)	North Dakota	8	48 (+96.2%)	29	50 (+26%)
Florida	47	2 (−22.0%)	28	1 (−25%)	Ohio	26	28 (−1.4%)	14	30 (+0.1%)
Georgia	41	5 (−16.6%)	27	5 (−17.8%)	Oklahoma	43	7 (−15.6%)	39	8 (−11.8%)
Hawaii	3	NA	51	22 (−3.3%)	Oregon	25	24 (−3.3%)	26	26 (−1.6%)
Idaho	37	4 (−18%)	48	6 (−16.8%)	Pennsylvania	24	42 (+7.8%)	5	40 (+5.4%)
Illinois	31	47 (+30.8%)	10	48(_18.1%)	Rhode Island	23	31 (+1.1%)	8	33 (+/6%)
Indiana	16	NA	40	27 (−1.5%)	South Carolina	33	13 (−11.9%	23	16 (−5.3%)
Iowa	20	40 (+4.9%)	24	38 (+4/9%)	South Dakota	50	14 (−11.8%)	16	25 (−2.1%)
Kansas	12	41 (+6.5%)	44	13 (−7.7%)	Tennessee	44	34 (+2.4%)	37	29 (−0.2%)
Kentucky	28	22 (−5.9%)	38	24 (−2.4%)	Texas	46	6 (−15.9%)	19	17 (−4.8%)
Louisiana	36	10 (−12.4%)	20	19 (−4.5%)	Utah	45	8 (−14.6%)	43	10 (−8.6%)
Maine	29	19 (−9%)	11	37 (+2/8%)	Vermont	1	44 (+15.5%)	50	47 (+14.7%)
Maryland	18	29 (−1.4%)	9	18 (−4.6%)	Virginia	40	18 (− 9.9%	15	12 (−8.1%)
Massachusetts	17	30 (+0.3%)	6	39 (+5.1%)	Washington	15	35 (+2.7%)	36	41 (+5/7%)
Michigan	14	21 (−7.4%)	30	9 (−9.9%)	Washington, DC	NA	NA	1	NA
Minnesota	6	32 (+1.5%)	32	36 (+2%)	West Virginia	19	38 (+3.6%)	35	42 (+5.7%)
Mississippi	42	9 (−12.4%)	42	15 (−5.7%)	Wisconsin	21	16 (−10.6%)	21	20 (−4.1%)
Missouri	39	39 (+ 4.2%)	17	32 (+0.4%)	Wyoming	4	43 (+8.5%)	13	34 (+0.8%)
Montana	3	NA	51	22 (−3.3%)					

Sources: Leachman et al. (2017) and U.S. Census Bureau (2019a).

state revenue from 2008 to 2016. The table also shows combined local and state per-pupil revenue ranks and percentage changes from 2008 to 2016 by jurisdiction.

State legislatures must recognize the effect that state budget cuts have on school districts in undermining public education operations, particularly the added stress on local property tax funding, financial uncertainty for schools in balancing district budgets, and impediments on education initiatives adopted by the state. When property assessments decline and property tax decreases, school officials must reduce student services to balance the budget or attempt to pass an excess levy in those states requiring such (Leachman et al., 2017).

When state or federal legislators choose to reduce district revenues, school leaders have very limited control over this decision, but they remain obligated to educate students at the same educational level as before reductions. Lawmakers, in many instances, expect schools to advance student academic performances, even with less financial state support than before the cuts.

ESCALATING COSTS

With declining revenue due to budget cuts and rising operational costs, public schools across much of the United States face fiscal distress with substantial challenges to balance district budgets. Some political rhetoric, however, often fosters the notion that schools can do "more with less money" during financially troubling times. In reality, many district costs are obligatory, ongoing, and escalating.

District costs soared well above the latest 2.9% annual rate (U.S. Department of Labor, 2018) in four key areas—employee healthcare insurance, pension assurance, special education services, and textbooks. Rising health insurance expenses in the United States are a national concern and spark vigorous policy debates. Soaring coverage costs remains a fiscal challenge for school districts with budgets squeezed by spiraling insurance expenses. Sisko et al. (2019) projected annual national healthcare expenses to expand 5.5% annually from 2019 to 2027.

In another area of concern, school district pension expenditures nationwide exhibit wide variations. Retirement expenditures in some states have not risen due to legal structural changes, such as modifying the retirement age (e.g., Ohio) or transferring costs onto the retiree (e.g., Wisconsin). District pension expenses in many states, however, doubled in the past decade due to a disproportionate number of retirees entering the system versus employees who contributed to the system. Substantial rocketing retiree healthcare costs caused districts extra expense too (Brainard & Brown, 2018).

To tackle these financial difficulties, lawmakers must adopt retirement policies that reduce the district liability instead of delaying ultimate expense hikes. In addition, policymakers in states who do not allow Social Security coverage for educators should revisit that decision from decades ago. With this change, Social Security could ease state lawmakers' stress on retirement policy decisions and afford primary and secondary public educators with a nationally portable retirement benefit (Schmitz & Aldeman, 2017).

Legislators, furthermore, should examine alternatives to pension plans for new workers without adding to the debt. Because 90% of educators currently received a defined benefit pension, lawmakers could create defined contribution, cash balance, or hybrid retirement plans as the default option for those educators. While neither the defined contribution, cash balance, nor hybrid plans will negate existing state or district pension debt, these arrangements may forestall future liabilities and allow educators more retirement flexibility (Schmitz & Aldeman, 2017).

Demand for special education services expanded much faster than state and federal support; thus, districts must allocate extra monies from local revenue to implement these mandated services. While the total number of students with special needs in the United States increased slightly from 6.8 million students in 2017 to 7 million in 2018, the number of students with a severe disorder increased significantly (McFarland et al., 2019). For instance, the estimated prevalence of children diagnosed with autism spectrum disorders showed an increase from one in 68 children in 2016 to one in 59 children in 2018. Autism spectrum disorder affects up to 3% of children in the United States (Christensen et al., 2019).

In addition, the number of students with other impairments (e.g., attention deficit and deficit hyperactivity disorders) increased 20% in the past five years (Snyder et al., 2019). Due to these changes, the average cost to educate students with special needs multiplied dramatically. Serving more children with severe disabilities often commands additional specialist services, unique equipment, and one-on-one aides, causing rising personnel costs with previously mentioned extra employee healthcare and pension expenses.

Although a number of states and the District of Columbia offered a weighted scale in basic aid or categorical funding to account for differences in educating children with varying special needs, the federal government does not distinguish different categories in the funding formula (Congressional Research Service, 2019). Federal lawmakers should enact legislation to differentiate students by disability and recognize different categories in the funding formula. This action could offset increased special education expenses.

To better finance children with special needs, lawmakers in those states without a weighted student scale should add specific disability classes in the basic aid or categorical formula. Legislators in states with few disability categories should differentiate more categories in the funding formulas. Due to the wide variance in disability service costs, weights directly associated with the cost to educate a student in a specific special education category allow states to deliver more apt, adequate funding than without appropriate weights.

Because most states do not collect detailed financial data on special education spending, state departments of education should collect authentic costs to educate students in varying categories. After verifying the definite cost to educate the various disability types, state departments of education should then compare true expenses per student by classification with allotted dollars. Based on these data, legislatures then should modify disability categories with a more realistic weighted formula to reflect actual costs in comparison to special education allocations.

Primary and secondary school textbook prices, another area for hiked costs, soared in recent years. Textbook expenditures are a financial burden for districts because 42 states and the District of Columbia provide free textbooks to students. Textbook costs have skyrocketed over the past several years with the average price increasing 88% between 2006 and 2016 (Berman, 2019).

Adding to the problem, 18 states select classroom textbooks at the state level, which inflates this expense out of the district's control. Publishers attribute higher prices due to employee salaries, logistics, and printing (Allen & Seaman, 2017; Thompson, 2017). Because electronic textbooks (e-books) cost less than print textbooks, purchasing e-books and/or using open educational resources can affect this elevated district expenditure (Boczar & Pascual, 2017).

To reduce budgets and corresponding appropriations, district actions as discussed in chapter 1 may reduce overall expenses. To mitigate group health and risk management insurances' spiraling costs, suggested actions in chapter 2 may reduce or contain district escalations. To effectively fund capital investments, processes mentioned in chapter 3 may better manage expenditures. To efficiently manage school district resources, school officials must vigilantly watch economic indicators and spending trends, particularly in specific expenditures that may surge above the normal inflation rate (e.g., bus fuel and utility costs).

UNFUNDED AND UNDERFUNDED MANDATES

Public education remains one of the most highly regulated governmental services commanded by federal and state laws, policies, and regulations. To meet these mandatory obligations, school districts must wisely spend money and invest time. When the federal or state government does not grant money to fulfill statutes or regulations, these legislative actions cause unfunded mandates. When the government specifies only a portion of the necessary funding to implement a statute or regulation, an underfunded mandate unfolds (Texas Association of Counties, 2019).

Mandates—both unfunded and underfunded—have a significant and direct effect on a district's budget. When federal or state legislation imposes an unfunded or underfunded mandate, the school district must implement the law and locally assume the expense. As a result, school districts must modify and/or reduce other appropriation lines, trim current programs and services, or increase local revenue to pay for the directive (Rubin, 2017).

Many federal orders are well-intended legislation; nevertheless, unfunded and underfunded mandates encompass

- mandated tests;
- fire and crisis management plans;
- child abuse and antibullying programs;
- vocation, charter, and nonpublic school students' transportation;
- building modifications and rectifications (e.g., asbestos removal);
- certificating, evaluating, hiring, training, mentoring, and terminating employees;
- student suspensions, expulsions, record maintenance, nutrition, truancy, and health mandates (e.g., defibrillators);
- special education services, including preschool for children with special needs; and
- Family and Medical Leave Act benefits (Texas Association of School Administrators and Texas Association of School Boards, 2018).

Special education services are the most expensive underfunded, highly controlled federal regulation. With the first federal special education law enacted in 1975, the U.S. Congress promised to cover 40% of the cost to implement mandatory special education services; however, the amount allotted by federal funding has been considerably less. The federal government, in fact, funded slightly over 10% of special education program costs through entitlements and Medicaid reimbursements (Arsen, Delpier, & Nagel, 2019).

With minimal federal government funding and escalated special education expenses, the continued commitment to fund students with special needs shifts to state governments and/or local school districts.

Legislatively unfunded and underfunded demands by states on districts may include

- audits and fiscal reports;
- staff collective bargaining regulations;

- student transportation;
- pension and workers' compensation programs;
- professional development in-service (e.g., concussion, child abuse, and antibullying training);
- building inspections, certifications, and prevailing wage expectations for construction projects;
- foster care and juvenile rehabilitation services; and
- statewide textbook adoptions (Maestas, 2017).

Although 35 states have a constitutional amendment or statutory provision to reimburse local governmental subdivisions, including school districts, for unfunded and underfunded mandates, state governments do not abide by the obligation. States avoid paying for dictates by simply ignoring statutory requirements due to the disproportionate power between the state government and local subdivisions (Rubin, 2017).

In response to unfunded and underfunded mandates, lawmakers should

- examine the cost of current unfunded and underfunded mandates,
- integrate current unfunded and underfunded mandates' implementation costs into appropriated state or federal aid,
- realize the burden that unfunded and underfunded mandates exhibit on the school budget,
- request and analyze cost studies related to directives before legislating a mandate, and
- abide by the mandate relief law when in force or pass a mandate relief law when not present in existing legislation.

School officials should undertake the following actions in relationship to unfunded and underfunded mandates:

- recommend a board resolution to prohibit federal and/or state unfunded and underfunded mandates when not already legislated,
- advocate for a state constitutional amendment or statutory provision to eliminate unfunded and underfunded commands when necessary,
- stay abreast of state statutes, federal laws, and court cases related to mandate relief law,
- monitor and report the financial impact of unfunded and underfunded orders on the school district via communications with constituents and legislators, and
- file a complaint for expense reimbursement against the state legislation when appropriate.

EQUITABLE AND ADEQUATE SCHOOL FUNDING

Equitable and adequate school funding quantities remain as pressing issues for state legislatures in school finance policies. In the broadest sense, theorists for equity funding propose that a state should equally fund a child's education regardless of their residency.

Equal student-to-teacher ratios, comparable teacher salaries, similar school buildings, and parallel support services denote equitable funding among school districts within states and around the country. The per-pupil funding level in one section of the country or a state, therefore, should reasonably compare with funding levels from another area. Although absolute equality is not practical due to regional differences, approximate spending equality should subsist in principle.

State finance policies to ensure an equal educational opportunity for every student in all districts are fundamental regardless of student and/or district demographics. Equitable opportunities improve educational outcomes for all students and reduce achievement gaps between demographic classes. Yet, the face of compelling evidence, many states have not passed school funding reforms to meet the needs of all students, especially those most vulnerable due to poverty, race, disability, or lack of English fluency (Baker et al., 2018).

Some researchers report "money does not matter" with regard to student achievement. Other scholars, however, find that "money does matter" because per-pupil spending levels greatly influence student learning, accessible resources, and instruction delivery processes (Baker et al., 2018).

With equity, a district's ability to generate local revenue via property tax in comparison to other districts is unfair in practice. In other words, does the state funding mechanism grant extra monies to districts with weak fiscal capacity, or is the state funding formula blind to a district's ability to raise local funds?

When state funding formula variables meritoriously substantiate the interaction between local and state revenues, equitable distribution levels may result. When imbalances exist, state-elected officials should sanction school finance reforms to bolster districts with a limited ability to raise the same local funds as districts with greater fiscal capacity (Baker et al., 2018).

Although a number of national reports analyzed state funding systems, the *National Report Card* by Baker et al. (2018) utilized exact state and local revenues at the district level to compare each state's primary and secondary public education funding. This report evaluated, compared, ranked, and graded each state on four funding fairness criteria to investigate children's equal educational opportunities.

The *National Report Card* (Baker et al., 2018) incorporated the following four fairness measurements with descriptions and analyses:

- The specific per-pupil funding level exhibited the absolute combined state and local revenue between states. This analysis revealed a wide funding disparity, with huge differences in students' educational opportunities. Per-pupil funding in Idaho, for example, was one-third less than the per-pupil revenue for a New York student.
- Funding distribution assessed per-pupil funding across districts within a state relative to students living in poverty. Utah, Delaware, and Minnesota, the most progressive states, granted districts with the highest concentration of household poverty more per-pupil funding than districts with a lower concentration of household poverty. Nevada, Illinois, and North Dakota, the most regressive states, awarded districts with a high concentration of students from poor families less than 75 cents for every per-pupil dollar compared to districts with a lower concentration of students from impoverished families.
- Fiscal effort reported the differences in state spending between elementary and secondary public school districts relative to the state's fiscal ability to fund districts. This variable evaluated a state's ability to fund districts according to state gross product (SGP) and aggregate personal income (API). Alaska, New Jersey, New Mexico, New York, Vermont, West Virginia, and Wyoming recorded an excellent fiscal effort in both standards, whereas Arizona, California, Colorado, Florida, Hawaii, Idaho, Indiana, Nevada, North Carolina, Oklahoma, South Dakota, Tennessee, and Washington documented a failing fiscal effort in both standards.
- Coverage surveyed the percentage of school-aged children enrolled in traditional public schools versus the percentage enrolled in nonpublic schools and then compared the average income differences between each set of households. When high-income families removed their children from primary and secondary public schools into nonpublic schools, a higher concentration of children from impoverished means remained in the public school. This circumstance, without funding allowances, aggravated equitable funding because the remaining students in public schools normally needed additional resources and services.

Regarding state specifics for coverage, Utah, Wyoming, and Maine ranked lowest in the United States with comparatively few students who opted out of public schools, and the families in these states whose children attended nonpublic schools were not economically different from the public school families. The District of Columbia, Louisiana, and Hawaii, on the other hand, ranked highest in the United States with a large percentage of students who did not attend public schools, and families with children in nonpublic schools were significantly wealthier than families whose children remained in public schools (Baker et al., 2018).

Baker et al. (2018) reported additional findings:

- New Jersey and Wyoming were the only states positioned relatively well on all four fairness indicators.
- Vermont and West Virginia ranked high on state fiscal effort and coverage, but these states rated poorly on important funding distribution measures. Even though these states had above-average funding levels and a relatively high fiscal effort, the distribution of funds disadvantaged high-poverty districts.
- Arizona, Nevada, South Dakota, and Texas ranked low on all measures except coverage.
- Colorado, North Carolina, and Utah progressively distributed funding systems, but these states maintained low funding levels. Without a sufficient funding level, even a reasonably progressive system cannot be fair. These states also rated low on fiscal effort, indicating that they had the capacity to increase basic aid, but the legislature did not increase funding for public schools.
- California, Florida, Louisiana, and Tennessee rated low on most measures—funding levels, fiscal effort, and fund distribution.

Table 4.4 displays the *National Report Card* ranks and grades (A–F) jurisdictions on the four fairness measures.

The *National Report Card* (Baker et al., 2018) also compared and ranked each state on three resource allocation indicators to investigate children's equal educational opportunities. These variables inspected each state's public education funding policy priorities, and the effect those policies had on students' quality and breadth of educational opportunities.

The *National Report Card* (Baker et al., 2018) descriptors and analyses of the three resource allocation indicators were as follows:

- Early childhood education examined the ratio of the percentage of students from low-income households enrolled in public preschool programs as compared with the percentage of enrolled preschool students who do not live with low-income families. Because children from low-income families often academically lag behind peers from high-income families, preschool programs aimed at children from low-income families can help reduce academic achievement gaps between groups. Jurisdictions that recognized the need for early intervention in a child's education focused funding to support and provide opportunities for children from low-income families.

Table 4.4 National Report Card State Ranks and Grades on Fairness Measures

Jurisdiction	Funding Level	Funding Distribution	Fiscal Effort		Coverage	Jurisdiction	Funding Level	Funding Distribution	Fiscal Effort		Coverage
			SGP	API					SGP	API	
Alabama	39	40 (F)	16 (B)	24 (C)	37	Nebraska	20	29 (C)	19 (C)	10 (B)	38
Alaska	2	NA	2 (A)	12 (A)	5	Nevada	42	48 (F)	46 (F)	45 (F)	13
Arizona	48	42 (F)	49 (F)	49 (F)	6	New Hampshire	11	34 (D)	14 (B)	29 (C)	12
Arkansas	36	9 (B)	8 (A)	15 (B)	22	New Jersey	5	5 (A)	4 (A)	5 (A)	25
California	32	16 (C)	44 (F)	42 (F)	31	New Mexico	33	37 (D)	12 (A)	6 (A)	17
Colorado	35	10 (B)	45 (F)	46 (F)	8	New York	1	31 (C)	5 (A)	3 (A)	41
Connecticut	6	32 (C)	24 (C)	33 (D)	30	North Carolina	47	12 (B)	48 (F)	44 (F)	33
Delaware	10	2 (A)	47 (F)	17 (C)	48	North Dakota	18	46 (F)	35 (F)	21 (C)	26
Florida	41	24 (C)	38 (F)	48 (F)	45	Ohio	15	4 (A)	18 (C)	11 (B)	40
Georgia	37	8 (B)	21 (C)	14 (B)	36	Oklahoma	45	17 (C)	33 (F)	41 (F)	10
Hawaii	NA	NA	50 (F)	50 (F)	49	Oregon	27	28 (C)	36 (F)	35 (D)	15
Idaho	49	23 (C)	37 (F)	47 (F)	9	Pennsylvania	8	25 (C)	15 (B)	16 (C)	35
Illinois	16	47 (F)	29 (C)	25 (C)	32	Rhode Island	9	35 (D)	9 (A)	9 (B)	42
Indiana	19	13 (C)	42 (F)	38 (F)	29	South Carolina	26	15 (C)	11 (A)	13 (B)	27
Iowa	17	33 (D)	20 (C)	8 (B)	7	South Dakota	40	43 (F)	39 (F)	40 (F)	14
Kansas	25	20 (C)	17 (C)	19 (C)	21	Tennessee	43	27 (C)	43 (F)	43 (F)	43
Kentucky	34	21 (C)	23 (C)	23 (C)	46	Texas	38	36 (D)	34 (F)	31 (C)	23
Louisiana	28	14 (C)	31 (C)	26 (C)	50	Utah	46	1 (A)	41 (F)	36 (D)	1
Maine	14	44 (F)	10 (A)	18 (C)	3	Vermont	2	22 (C)	1 (A)	4 (A)	11
Maryland	12	38 (D)	27 (C)	32 (D)	47	Virginia	29	41 (F)	30 (C)	4 (D)	28
Massachusetts	7	7 (A)	32 (D)	37 (D)	18	Washington	22	30 (C)	40 (F)	39 (F)	24
Michigan	24	26 (C)	25 (C)	30 (C)	19	Washington, DC	NA	NA	NA	NA	51
Minnesota	13	3 (A)	26 (C)	22 (C)	20	West Virginia	21	18 (C)	7 (A)	7 (A)	4
Mississippi	44	19 (C)	6 (A)	12 (B)	44	Wisconsin	16	11 (B)	22 (C)	20 (C)	34
Missouri	31	45 (F)	28 (C)	28 (C)	39	Wyoming	4	6 (A)	3 (A)	2 (A)	2
Montana	30	39 (D)	13 (B)	27 (C)	16						

Source: Baker et al. (2018).

- Teacher-to-student ratios compared proportions of staff members in poverty-poor districts against proportions of staff members in poverty-rich districts. For instance, poverty-poor districts in North Dakota had 40% more teachers per 100 students than property-rich districts, resulting in smaller teacher-to-student ratios at property-poor districts than teacher-to-student ratios at property-rich schools. Florida, in contrast, had 25% fewer teachers per 100 students in poverty-poor districts than property-rich districts, which indicated smaller teacher-to-student ratios and expanded services for property-rich districts. A high teacher-to-student proportional ratio in poverty-poor districts recognized that additional resources and staff members (e.g., math specialists, instructional coaches, counselors, and nurses) were necessary to educate children from low-income families.
- Wage competitiveness compared the average compensation, education level, experience, and working hours of public schoolteachers to the same variables for the average nonteaching professional.

Based on the early childhood education ratio, Baker et al. (2018) found that public early childhood education program enrollments in South Dakota, Wyoming, Vermont, and Montana for children living in low-income households were more likely than similar enrollments for children from high-income households.

To the contrary, public early childhood education program enrollments in Alaska, Maine, North Dakota, and West Virginia for students from low-income families were less likely than similar enrollments for children from high-income families. Public preschool participation rates in these states illustrated unequal educational opportunities because only one-third of preschool children from low-income families accessed a public early childhood education program. In the vast majority of states, enrollments in public preschools for children from low-income families were considerably lower than similar enrollments for children from high-income families (Baker et al., 2018).

Regarding teacher-to-student ratios, districts with a high concentration of low-income families in North Dakota had 40% more teachers per 100 students than districts with a low concentration of low-income families, resulting in smaller teacher-to-student ratios at districts with a high concentration of low-income families than at schools with a low concentration of low-income families. Florida, by contrast, had 25% fewer teachers per 100 students in districts with a high concentration of low-income families than districts with a low concentration of low-income families, resulting in smaller teacher-to-student ratios at districts with a low concentration of low-income families. A lower proportionate teacher-to-student ratio for districts with a high concentration of low-income families than districts with a low concentration of low-income families recognized that additional resources and staff members (e.g., math specialists, instructional coaches, counselors, and nurses) were necessary to educate students from low-income families (Baker et al., 2018).

Regarding wage competitiveness between teachers and nonteaching professionals, Baker et al. (2018) found that the average teacher salary in most states was far below the average nonteaching professionals' compensation. Arizona, Kansas, and Wyoming showed the least disparity between teachers and nonteaching professionals' wages, whereas Colorado, New Hampshire, and Virginia revealed the greatest disparity. To ensure that teaching positions remain desirable in the job market, a competitive wage is fundamental for a district's ability to attract and retain high-quality teachers, which may result in more equitable schools than in states without a competitive wage.

Based on these allocation ranks and resource indicators, the *National Report Card* showed wide disparities in state allocations for student resources to ensure equal educational opportunities at primary and secondary public school districts across the United States. Table 4.5 illustrates the *National Report Card* allocation ranks by jurisdiction and resource indicators.

To examine equity in state funding distribution systems, the following variables in each state's basic aid funding equalize monies—district concentrated poverty (DCP) and student weights, such as low-income (LIW), disability (DW), and English language learner (ELLW).

The Education Commission of the States (2018b) study acknowledged jurisdictions' funding for concentrated district poverty as well as student low income. The study also examined student disbility weights and identified special education jurisdiction formula, category, or staff-based funding. Parker, Diffey, and Atchison (2016, 2018) recorded jurisdiction funding for prekindergarten (preK) and full-day kindergarten (FDK) programs across the United States. Acknowledging the factors from these sources categorizes equitable funding distributions in jurisdiction funding systems.

For instance, a fair state funding formula distributes more dollars to districts with concentrated poverty and assigns additional student weights for children who live in poverty and need extra academic support. Twenty-eight states (see table 4.6) distinguished a district's concentrated poverty by family income as a variable in jurisdiction funding whether in the formula or categorical aid. Twenty-one states recognized an additional student weight for children from low-income families in the funding formula (Education Commission of the States, 2018b). A funding system that distinguishes student and district poverty characteristics within formula variables may remedy funding

Table 4.5 National Report Card Allocation Ranks by Resource Indicator

Jurisdiction	*Early Childhood Ratio*	*Teacher-to-Student Ratio*	*Competitive Wages*	*Jurisdiction*	*Early Childhood Ratio*	*Teacher-to-Student Ratio*	*Competitive Wages*
Alabama	39	35	38	Nebraska	43	16	25
Alaska	46	6	3 (tie)	Nevada	9	No Data	14
Arizona	45	33	45	New Hampshire	42	3	50
Arkansas	8	9	12	New Jersey	15	21	10
California	27	30	34	New Mexico	11	18	20
Colorado	16	4	51	New York	12	42	17
Connecticut	22	45	40	North Carolina	35	23	41
Delaware	34	13	35	North Dakota	51	1	28
Florida	29	48	39	Ohio	23	36	18
Georgia	21	25	46	Oklahoma	17	11	36
Hawaii	49	No Data	13	Oregon	33	34	26
Idaho	6	14	9	Pennsylvania	30	44	4
Illinois	25	43	16	Rhode Island	46	46	5
Indiana	37	39	23	South Carolina	28	26	37
Iowa	18	19	3 (tie)	South Dakota	1	5	7
Kansas	31	12	31	Tennessee	38	27	42
Kentucky	26	17	8	Texas	32	32	43
Louisiana	13	47	27	Utah	24	37	48
Maine	50	40	21	Vermont	3	7	6
Maryland	36	41	19	Virginia	47	28	49
Massachusetts	40	24	22	Washington	44	15	47
Michigan	19	22	30	Washington, DC	10	No Data	29
Minnesota	14	2	24	West Virginia	41	20	33
Mississippi	5	31	32	Wisconsin	7	38	11
Missouri	20	29	44	Wyoming	2	8	1
Montana	4	10	15				

Source: Baker et al. (2018).

disparities between students from low- and high-income families and students from low- and high-concentrated poverty districts.

Weighting students by specific category identifies students who exhibit special learning needs and directs extra money to educate these students. Twenty-three states and the District of Columbia recognized special education students in the state basic aid funding formula (F), with 13 of those jurisdictions assigning multiple DWs within the formula. Fourteen states funded special education with categorical (C) funding, seven states reimbursed (R) districts for special education costs, and five states subsidized special education resources by staff (S). Connecticut does not provide any additional special education funding for school districts (Education Commission of the States, 2018b).

Thirty-two states and the District of Columbia recognized English language learner weights in the funding formula (F), the most common distinction. Ten states provided categorical (C) funding for English language learners (ELL), two states allocated ELL funding by staff (S), four states reimbursed (R) districts for ELL, and two states did not offer funding for ELL students (Education Commission of the States, 2018b). With categorical or reimbursement ELL funding, the state allocation remains subject to legislative discretion and easily eligible for targeted cuts.

Establishing weights for student populations with special necessities equalize educational opportunities because these students generally present more expensive education needs than typically developing youngsters. Eight states and the District of Columbia provided funding for preK programs within the basic aid formula, and 13 states and the District of Columbia funded FDK programs (Parker et al., 2016, 2018). Granting extra funding for these programs fosters equality and may close academic achievement gaps between student groups.

Table 4.6 displays a summary of variables in basic aid formulas, by jurisdiction, to support equity allocations based on unique district and student characteristics.

The *National Report Card* (Baker et al., 2018) reported irrefutable evidence that most basic aid finance systems failed to provide all children across the United States with an equal opportunity for educational success. This study supported school finance reforms to tackle funding inequalities.

Adequate school funding, another key fiscal measurement, examines a jurisdiction's commitment to grant districts sufficient per-pupil funding for attaining all students' minimal proficiencies on distinct standards. Adequate school funding confounds analysts because per-pupil revenue for traditional public education is easily quantified; however, the necessary cost to educate a child with a sufficient per-pupil revenue level to meet academic standards

Table 4.6 Basic Aid Formula Variables

Jurisdiction	*DCP*	*LIW*	*DW*	*ELLW*	*PreK*	*FDK*	*Jurisdiction*	*DCP*	*LIW*	*DW*	*ELLW*	*PreK*	*FDK*
Alabama	X		S	C		X	Nebraska	X		R	F (1)		
Alaska	None	None	F (1)	F (1)			Nevada		X (1)	C	C		
Arizona	None	None	F (14)	F (1)			New Hampshire	X		F (1)	F (1)		
Arkansas	X		C	F		X	New Jersey	X		C	F (1)		
California	X	X (1)	C	F (1)			New Mexico	X		F (4)	F (1)		
Colorado	X	X (2)	C	C (2)	X		New York	X		F (1)	F (1)		
Connecticut		X (1)	None	C			North Carolina	X		C	F (1)		X
Delaware	None	None	S	R		X	North Dakota		X (1)	F (1)	F (3)		
Florida	C		F (5)	F (1)			Ohio	X		F (6)	C		
Georgia		X	F (5)	F (1)			Oklahoma		X (1)	F (10)	F (1)	X	X
Hawaii		X (1)	C	F (4)			Oregon		X (1)	F (1)	F (1)		
Idaho	None	None	S	C			Pennsylvania	X		C (3)	C		
Illinois	X	X	C	R			Rhode Island	X		R	F (1)		X
Indiana	C		F (5)	C			South Carolina	X		F (10)	F (1)		X
Iowa	X		F (3)	F (1)	X		South Dakota	None	None	F (6)	F (1)		
Kansas	X		F (1)	F (1)			Tennessee	X		S	F (1)		X
Kentucky		X (1)	F (3)	F (1)			Texas	X		F (6)	F (1)	X	
Louisiana		X	F (1)	F (1)		X	Utah	C		C	C		
Maine		X	F (3)	F (3)	X		Vermont	X		R	F (1)	X	
Maryland		X (1)	F (1)	F (1)		X	Virginia	X	X (2)	S	S		
Massachusetts		X (1)	C	F (2)			Washington	X		F (1)	F (2)		X
Michigan		X (1)	R	R			Washington, DC			F (5)	F (1)	X	X
Minnesota		X (1)	C	F (1)			West Virginia	X		C	C	X	X
Mississippi		X (1)	S	None		X	Wisconsin	C		R	R	X	
Missouri		X	F (1)	F (1)			Wyoming	X		R	S		
Montana		X	C	None									

Sources: Education Commission of the States (2018) and Parker et al. (2016, 2018).

is much more difficult to quantify than per-pupil funding levels (Alexander & Alexander, 2019; Barba et al., 2016).

Adequacy cost studies attempt to empirically measure the estimated cost of primary and secondary public education to achieve specific student outcomes. Over 30 states performed adequacy cost studies driven by court interventions. State and the District of Columbia legislatures, on occasion, request an adequacy cost study to allocate elementary and secondary public education dollars before court involvement (Odden & Picus, 2020).

Researchers have applied four methodologies (e.g., professional judgment, evidence-based, successful school/district, and cost function) to assess the aggregate cost of a satisfactory primary and secondary public education, including essential expenses, specific resources, and dollar values for precise services (Brimley et al., 2020; Odden & Picus, 2020).

The professional judgment approach employs the ability of experienced educational experts to specify necessary costs, resources (e.g., personnel, class size, materials, supplies, technology, utilities, and equipment), and quantities (i.e., number of teachers) for a satisfactory education to meet standards, educational goals, and legal qualifications. Although this per-pupil cost approach is easy to understand and relatively transparent, this objective, bottom-up method does not evaluate fund distribution methodologies. This approach, often coupled with an evidence-based approach, simply addresses fund shortcomings and does not examine the means in distributing the funds (Brimley et al., 2020; Odden & Picus, 2020).

The evidence-based approach relies on current educational research findings to clarify the essential resources for a prototypical school to meet the state's student performance benchmarks. After distinguishing evidence-based strategies (i.e., optimal teacher ratio per assigned elementary students), this method attaches a cost for each variable and then aggregately combines variables to quantify a satisfactory school site, total expenses, and the state funding level to meet educational needs (Odden & Picus, 2020).

This approach, however, does not include certain school management properties into the calculation because expenses, such as central office costs, do not have a research value. State legislatures, on occasion prior to court interventions, utilize evidence-based expenditure levels to ascertain the necessary state basic aid dollars for primary and secondary public education (Brimley et al., 2020).

From 2003 to the present, Arizona, Arkansas, Kentucky, Maine, Maryland, Michigan, North Dakota, Ohio, Texas, Vermont, Washington, Wisconsin, and Wyoming employed the evidence-based strategy (Picus, Odden, & Associates, 2019).

The successful school/district approach estimates the cost of a satisfactory elementary and secondary public education based on schools and/or districts that successfully fulfilled student expectations (e.g., standardized test scores and graduation rates). The successful school/district approach effectively specifies the spending level linked to student performance. This method, however, does not indicate how districts should spend funds to produce successful student achievement. This approach often eliminates atypical districts (e.g., city, large, small, and rural districts) from the study (Brimley et al., 2020; Odden & Picus, 2020).

The econometric, cost function approach relies on statistical analyses to estimate costs that correlate sufficient per-pupil spending with desired student achievements. Odden and Picus (2020) confirm that this process produces an adequate per-pupil expenditure for an average district and then adjusts the findings for districts using complex statistical calculations, such as student characteristics (e.g., special needs and children from low-income families) and district qualities (e.g., city, large, small, rural, and concentrated poverty). Although this method remains popular among economists, the approach is difficult to explain to policymakers and the community due to the mathematical complexities.

Experts conducted cost function studies in California, Illinois, New York, Texas, and Wisconsin, although each state exercised different input variables and varying definitions for satisfactory student performance. Results, in general, disclosed substantial variations in average expenses and district needs. As performance expectations rise, expenditure costs generally increase (Odden & Picus, 2020).

Despite the growing sophistication of researchers' efforts to measure associated costs for a satisfactory primary and secondary public education, the processes remain inconclusive because cost estimates occur in a prejudiced and often litigious atmosphere. Political motives and differing judgments frequently cloud findings; therefore, these studies yield confusing and contested data because each method possesses unique philosophical or methodological flaws (Odden & Picus, 2020).

Researchers in the future must scientifically extend studies to identify costs related to first-rate learning and teaching, such as constructive learner prototypes, supportive teacher behaviors, productive interactions between the student and teacher, favorable educational settings, and beneficial curricular materials. As accountability intensifies, exploring atmospheres in learning environments and converting those specific patterns to definite positive student academic achievement may lead to more conclusive studies with precise costs for suitable children's education.

When lawmakers do not appropriately address adequate or equitable school funding, state courts intervene. Because equity and adequacy standards in financing elementary and secondary public schools legally derive from equal protection clauses in state constitutions, litigation at the state level modified the public education finance systems more often than any other public service in the past three decades (Alexander & Alexander, 2019).

Between 1973 and 2018, plaintiffs in 36 states contested the state funding method based on constitutional equal protection clauses (i.e., equity grounds), and 37 states disputed the system on adequacy grounds. In rulings from Alaska, Arkansas, Idaho, Kansas, Kentucky, New Jersey, Ohio, South Carolina, and Washington, each state's supreme court ordered legislatures to restructure financial processes with less reliance on local property wealth and/or to deliver additional funding to meet constitutional standards (Hunter, 2018).

Mixed state supreme court verdicts in five states adjudicated opposing outcomes. Supreme courts in these states ordered legislative funding advancements in one case but upheld the system in another case (Hunter, 2018). Primary and secondary public education funding in Hawaii, Mississippi, Nevada, and Utah has never contested (Hunter, 2018; SchoolFunding.Info, 2019). To see state education finance litigation from 1973 to 2018, click or search for the SchoolFunding.Info website at http://schoolfunding.info/litigation-map and click on a state.

State supreme courts are best suited to enforce cost study findings. State court judges should

- demand that the exact cost of an adequate public education be regulated through a professional cost study;
- issue a simple, direct mandate that cost studies be transparent, involve public engagement, and set clear timelines for completion and execution;
- scrutinize the validity of the designated cost study methodology and request rigorous research on costs to meet state educational standards;
- utilize explicit, transparent, and analytic decision-making processes to justify each element of the contested funding formula;
- hold the state legislature accountable to execute court orders within a prescribed timetable;
- enforce remedies ordered by the court, particularly with phased-in solutions;
- monitor the reform and command necessary corrections; and
- ensure ongoing, regular cost study analyses.

In order to ensure and distribute adequate and equitable elementary and secondary public education basic aid, according to Chingos and Blagg (2017) and Parker et al. (2016, 2018), state lawmakers should

- honor the state's constitutional, statutory, and/or court orders for adequate and equitable funding;
- cast aside past political dealings that perpetuate inequitable funding;

- solicit experts in the field to scientifically measure an adequate and equitable preK–12 per-pupil funding level based on student academic performance standards;
- factor district fiscal capacity into the basic aid formula;
- authorize a district concentrated poverty variable when nonexistent;
- enact weights for students from low-income families, English language learners, and children with special needs based on the state department of education spending report when not already present;
- legislate prekindergarten and full-day kindergarten programs as variables when not already funded;
- assign per-pupil basic aid on the true cost to educate students in meeting constitutional and court directives;
- establish and follow comprehensive, timely accountability procedures; and
- deliver adequate, equitable basic aid via a creditable funding formula before court intervention.

For an adequate, equitable basic aid formula, school officials should

- keep abreast of state legislative actions and litigations;
- understand the strengths and weaknesses of adequacy cost approaches;
- advocate for a district concentrated poverty variable when nonexistent;
- promote justifiable weights for students from low-income families, English language learners, and children with special needs by category when nonexistent;
- maintain records and report resource allocations that link student weights and program expenditures with student academic outcomes;
- endorse preschool and full-day kindergarten program funding when nonexistent; and
- advocate intently for adequate and equitable school funding.

Satisfying a wide range of constituencies in the quest for an equitable, adequate elementary and secondary public education funding system is an ongoing political challenge for lawmakers because of the magnitude, scope, and difficulty to change existing systems. School finance systems that account for the essential elements to support equal educational opportunities with sufficient dollars related to student academic performance retain tremendous merit.

FUNDING CHALLENGES FOR NONPUBLIC AND PUBLIC CHARTER SCHOOLS

Nonpublic and public charter schools also face funding challenges. Nonpublic and charter schools, similar to public schools, must be concerned with equitable and adequate funding, escalating costs, and unfunded as well as underfunded mandates.

Nonpublic Schools

Parochial schools, most specifically, may reap positive benefits from future disputes in state courts regarding Blaine amendments that block public funding support for religious schools. As a result of the U.S. Supreme Court recently sending three cases back to their respective state supreme courts (i.e., Colorado, Missouri, and New Mexico), future state court disputes that oppose Blaine amendments may add public monies to support parochial schools (Weiner & Green, 2018). Although the Colorado Supreme Court dismissed the *Taxpayers for Public Education* case, the U.S. Supreme Court may reconsider Blaine amendments in the context of school choice (Carlson, 2018).

After *Zelman v. Simmons-Harris* (2002) upheld public monies for parochial schools and children through voucher programs funded by the state, the District of Columbia and 15 states (Arkansas, Florida, Georgia, Indiana, Louisiana, Maine, Maryland, Mississippi, New Hampshire, North Carolina, Ohio, Oklahoma, Utah, Vermont, and Wisconsin) grant public dollars for vouchers in some form to nonpublic schools (EdChoice, 2019). States currently without a voucher program should consider future endeavors.

Eight states (Alabama, Illinois, Indiana, Iowa, Louisiana, Minnesota, South Carolina, and Wisconsin) offer nonpublic school parents an individual income tax credit for a partial reimbursement of paid taxes. Tax credit scholarships in 18 states (Alabama, Arizona, Florida, Georgia, Illinois, Indiana, Iowa, Kansas, Louisiana Montana, Nevada, New Hampshire, Oklahoma, Pennsylvania, Rhode Island, South Carolina, South Dakota, and Virginia) permitted both individuals and corporations to claim a tax credit to support elementary and secondary nonpublic student scholarships, tuition, fees, or other related services. As a result, states presently without tax credits should consider permitting such an option (EdChoice, 2019).

To allocate equitable and adequate funding for nonpublic schools, lawmakers should reexamine and eliminate antiquated Blaine amendments in those states that block religious schools from receiving public funds. States without voucher and tax credit programs should pass legislation to advance equal educational opportunities for nonpublic school students.

To advocate for equitable and adequate school funding in nonpublic schools, school officials should

- campaign and dialogue for the abolition of Blaine amendments in those states enforcing such laws;

- support legislation in those states that do not possess permissive public funding laws;
- back political candidates who support state monies in nonpublic schools for vouchers, textbooks, auxiliary health and counseling services, statewide testing, transportation, professional development, technology, and other secular purposes; and
- encourage tax credit legislation that permits individuals and corporations to deduct elementary and secondary nonpublic student tuition and scholarship donations from their state income tax obligation when not already ratified.

Public Charter Schools

Funding public charter schools find similar concerns as funding traditional public schools with state budget reductions as well as unfunded and underfunded mandates. Because Montana, Nebraska, North Dakota, South Dakota, Vermont, and West Virginia do not authorize public charter schools, these state legislatures may reconsider this exclusion in the future with appropriated state funding.

Because the Louisiana Supreme Court decision upheld the constitutionality of state funding for public charter schools in the same manner as traditional public schools, other state courts may decree to allot public charter school dollars in the same methods as traditional public schools when not already available (O'Brien, Blessey-Bickford, & Grand, 2018).

Although public charter school supporters have argued that financing these schools improve efficiency and lower costs without compromising outcomes, the Center for Popular Democracy (2017) revealed that public charter school officials in 15 states have mismanaged over $223 million since 1994.

The researchers also verified cases of fraud, waste, and abuse due to inadequate internal controls over basic fiscal operations, blemished procurement procedures (i.e., competitive bidding), and inconsistent or inaccurate purchasing procedures (Center for Popular Democracy, 2017). With future revelations about abuse and misuse of taxpayer monies by charter school personnel, state legislatures may pass laws that subject charter schools to the same financial transparency and accountability standards as those mandated for public schools.

To allocate equitable and adequate funding for charter schools, lawmakers should

- approve legislation to form charter schools in those states without such legislation,
- appropriate state charter school funding in the same manner as conventional primary and secondary public schools in states without similar practices,

- revise laws to command charter schools to operate within the same regulations (e.g., competitive bid law) as traditional elementary and secondary public schools,
- hold charter school sponsors and operators accountable for funding audits in the same manner as traditional public schools, and
- employ unbiased research regarding student outcomes and related charter schooling costs.

To advocate for equitable and adequate school funding in charter schools, school leaders should

- support charter school legislation in states without such laws,
- advocate for appropriated funding in the same manner as traditional elementary and secondary public schools,
- encourage legislation that compels charter schools to adhere to the same regulations as traditional elementary and secondary public schools, and
- promote laws that oblige charter schools to be accountable to the state government in the same vein as traditional public schools.

SUMMARY

School finance policy across the United States portrays complex historical, political, and economic conditions aggravated by confounding taxation systems to fund elementary and secondary public education. Sorting through research facts and myths to filter political biases regarding taxation and school finance policies can be demanding. Those individuals interested in tax and school finance reform must develop keen analytical skills to evaluate current and future strategies (Brimley et al., 2020).

At the heart of American school finance is the taxation system, which some tax experts depicted as egregiously unfair to low- and middle-income families (Wiehe et al., 2018). Restructuring existing tax systems that align with today's needs could result in understandable, efficient strategies to tax individuals and corporations more fairly. Just tax systems foster support for public services, including primary and secondary public education (Barba et al., 2016).

Because of varying funding sources, intricacies, and complex elements, school funding is neither transparent nor explicable (Baker et al., 2018; Barba et al., 2016). When the public who frequently must approve school funds better understands school funding distribution methods than currently in custom, they may be more apt to accept increases than without comprehension.

Due to revenue issues in many states and rising operational costs over time, public schools across much of the United States have faced financial struggles to achieve student academic standards. State supreme courts in many instances have directed legislatures to revise finance systems, resulting in more equitable and adequate funding.

Over the past two decades, courts have relied on professional cost studies to confirm the exact financial commitment legislatures should grant elementary and secondary public education. These cost studies, conducted in more than 30 states, often replaced backroom political deals that previously dictated public education allocations, without any evidence to support the appropriation.

Although a single method may not estimate the precise cost of an adequate education, states applied four universally accepted approaches—professional judgment, evidence-based, successful school/district, and cost function. Allocating elementary and secondary public education funds with cost study processes offers better transparency and scientific reasoning than unvalidated legislative efforts. Researchers, however, should investigate supplementary teaching and learning variables for future expense analyses.

In order to fund schools sufficiently and administer funds resourcefully, everyone (i.e., lawmakers, school administrators, and the public) must share responsibility. Politicians must regulate just tax means on citizens to fund preK—12 educational services and establish equitable and adequate funding levels via formulas based on apt research.

School administrators and educators who deliver educational services must be aware of funding means and work within designated methods to provide the best quality education for all children. Despite continuous attention for educational reform by politicians and academic scholars, limited research constitutes optimal resource utilization to foster higher learning outcomes for all children.

Unfunded and underfunded mandates cause difficulty for school administrators to balance the budget. Lawmakers should calculate existing plus future unfunded and underfunded mandates' costs and allocate funding accordingly. When mandate relief laws exist, legislators should obey the law, and courts should enforce the law. When such legislation does not exist, states should authorize the proposition.

At parochial schools, three phenomena may alter the future of American school finance—Blaine amendment court disputes, voucher programs, and tax credits. Future litigation against state Blaine amendments that block public funds for schools supported by churches may increase funding for parochial schools.

Voucher legislation that allows public dollars to follow students directly to a nonpublic school for tuition will increase nonpublic school funding in those states that do not have a voucher program. When permitted, state and federal income tax credits for nonpublic school tuition and student scholarships will further children's nonpublic educational opportunities.

Regarding charter school funding, legislators may consider funding in the same format as traditional elementary and secondary public schools. Lawmakers may also legislate that charter schools adhere to the same laws as traditional schools. Due to illegal and improper fund management, legislators may hold charter schools more accountable than previous practices.

According to Mark Yudof (1991), renowned law professor and university administrator, as opined in jest by a pessimist, "school finance reform is like a Russian novel: it's long, tedious, and everybody dies in the end" (pg. 499).

PROJECTS

1. Study your district and/or building line-item appropriations and identify those expenditures that show escalating costs beyond the typical 3% inflation rate. Create a plan to address line items with increases higher than 5% and share your findings with colleagues, staff, fellow administrators, and school board members.
2. Review your state's school funding equity and adequacy lawsuits on the SchoolFunding.Info website at http://schoolfunding.info/litigation-map. Report the final ruling and the processes to determine whether the state was equitably and/or adequately funding districts.
3. To better understand adequacy cost studies, a group of peers should

    a. reach consensus on appropriate academic achievement measurements for students before graduation,
    b. brainstorm potential programs/resources for a school to achieve academic success for all students,
    c. examine each adequacy cost study's advantages and disadvantages, and
    d. select, by consensus, approaches that best fit the group's educational perspectives and philosophies.

4. When your jurisdiction concludes the next budget cycle, ascertain whether the new elementary and secondary public education appropriation increased or decreased from the previous budget and assess the distribution formula with regard to adequacy and equity funding provisions.
5. Compile a list of unfunded as well as underfunded mandates for your school district and examine the cost of each corresponding appropriation line. Report your findings.
6. With a coalition, investigate the taxation system of a jurisdiction by retrieving data from tables 4.1 and 4.2. Devise a sound tax policy position in light

of this chapter's content with specific recommendations to strengthen your jurisdiction's taxation system for the public good. Share the findings with community members, colleagues, staff, fellow administrators, and school board members.

7. With a coalition, create a funding distribution profile for your jurisdiction by retrieving and analyzing the data from tables 4.3 to 4.6. Design a school finance policy position in light of this chapter's content and share the findings with colleagues, staff, fellow administrators, and school board members.

References

Abrahams, D. L., & Motz, J. S. (2019, May). *Processing and evaluating bids.* PowerPoint presentation at the Michigan School Business Officials annual conference, Grand Rapids, Michigan.

Aegis Risk. (2019). *2019 Aegis risk medical stop loss premium survey.* Alexandria, VA: Author.

Aldeman, C., & Rotherham, A. J. (2019). *Teacher pension plans: How they work, and how they affect recruitment, retention, and equity.* Washington, DC: Bellwether Education Partners.

Alexander, K., & Alexander, F. K. (2019). *American public school law* (9th ed.). St. Paul, MN: West Academic.

Allen, I. E., & Seaman, J. (2017). *What we teach: K-12 school district curriculum adoption process, 2017.* Babson Park, MA: Babson Survey Research Group.

Alliant Insurance Services. (2019). *Insurance requirements in contracts: A procedure manual-2019 version.* Newport Beach, CA: Author.

Alvarado, D., & Quinn, B. (2018). *Managing worker's compensation costs.* San Francisco, CA: Edgewood Partners Insurance Center.

American Gaming Association. (2019). *State of the states 2018: The AGA survey of the commercial casino industry.* Washington, DC: Author.

American Recovery and Reinvestment Act, 42 U.S.C. §17921 (2009).

American Society of Civil Engineers. (2017). *2017 infrastructure report card.* Baltimore, MD: Author.

Andersson, F., Jordahl, H., & Josephson, J. (2019). Outsourcing public services: Contractibility, cost, and quality. *CESifo Economic Studies, 65*(4), 349–372.

Anthem Blue Cross and Blue Shield. (2019). *2018 National health benefits statistics & trends report.* Indianapolis, IN: Author.

Arial, C. M. (2019). *Public administrator choice Idaho school district finance policy observed* (Unpublished doctoral dissertation). Boise State University, Boise.

Arsen, D., Delpier, T., & Nagel, J. (2019). *Michigan school finance at the crossroads: A quarter century of state control.* Lansing Michigan State University.

Association of School Business Officials International. (2019). *International school business management professional standards and code of ethics*. Reston, VA: Author.

Avi-Yonah, R. S. (2006). The three goals of taxation. *Tax Law Review*, *60*(1), 1–28.

Baker, B. D. (2018). *Educational inequality and school finance: Why money matters for America's students*. Cambridge, MA: Harvard Education Press.

Baker, B. D., Di Carlo, M., & Weber, M. (2019). *The adequacy and fairness of state school finance systems*. Washington, DC: Albert Shanker Institute.

Baker, B. D., Farrie, D., & Sciarra, D. (2018). *Is school funding fair? A national report card* (7th ed.). Newark, NJ: Education Law Center.

Ballotpedia. (2019). *School bond and tax elections*. Retrieved from https://ballotpedia.org/Voting_on_school_bond_and_tax_measures.

Barba, M., Ginn, V., Grusendorf, K., & Heflin, T. (2016). *Texas school finance: Basics and reform*. Austin: TX: Texas Public Policy Foundation.

Beardsley, K., Cowen, C., Fiddemon, R., Morrision, S., O'Connor, J., Regan, B., & Scarcella, A. (2017). *Reference guide to instructional material aids*. Castleton, NY: Questar III Board of Cooperative Educational Services.

Beck, D., Watson, A. R., & Maranto, R. (2019). Do testing conditions explain cyber charter schools' failing grades? *American Journal of Distance Education*, *33*(1), 46–58.

Bell, K., & Orem, T. (2019, September 5). Estate tax: Definition, tax rates and who pays in 2019. Retrieved from https://www.nerdwallet.com/blog/taxes/which-states-have-estate-inheritance-taxes/.

Berman, J. (2019, May 9). *What the McGraw-Hill, Cengage merger means for textbook prices*. Retrieved from https://www.marketwatch.com/story/mcgraw-hill-and-cengage-are-merging-what-that-means-for-college-textbook-prices-2019–05–02.

Bhuvaneswaran, S. (2018, November 28). *For the last time: "Procurement" and "purchasing" are different*. Retrieved from https://kissflow.com/procurement-process/procurement-vs-purchasing/.

Biedron, R. (2018a). *Benefits of procurement technology and tools*. Framingham, MA: Purchase Control.

Biedron, R. (2018b). *Centralized vs. decentralized purchasing*. Framingham, MA: Purchase Control.

Boczar, J., & Pascual, L. (2017). E-books for the classroom and open access textbooks: Two ways to help students save money on textbooks. *The Serials Librarian*, *72*(1–4), 95–101.

Brainard, K., & Brown, A. (2018). *Significant reforms to state retirement systems*. Lexington, KY: National Association of State Retirement Administrators.

Brimley, V., Verstegen, D. A., & Knoeppel, R. C. (2020). *Financing education in a climate of change* (13th ed.). Boston, MA: Pearson.

Brookshire, J. (2015). Civil liability for bullying: How federal statutes and state tort law can protect our children. *Cumberland Law Review*, *45*(2), 351–394.

Bruno, P. (2019, May 6). School districts must do more to manage costs of health benefits. Retrieved from https://edsource.org/2019/school-districts-must-do-more-to-manage-costs-of-health-benefits/612025.

Burnette II, D. (July 17, 2019). Many unknowns in K-12 spending. *Education Week, 38*(37), 1–21.

Burnside, B. (2016). *Umbrella/excess liability insurance*. Brookfield, WI: T. E. Brennan Company.

California Office of Public School Construction. (2019). *School facility program handbook*. West Sacramento, CA: Author.

Calkins, K. J., & Convey, J. J. (2019). Seminarian sentiments about Catholic schools. *Journal of Catholic Education, 22*(1), 112–134.

Carlson, B. (2018). *Taxpayers for Public Education v. Douglas County School District*: The school choice movement solders on. *University of Colorado Law Review, 89*(4), 1273–1309.

Center for Connected Health Policy. (2019). *State telehealth laws & reimbursement policies*. Sacramento, CA: Author.

Center for Popular Democracy. (2017). *Charter school vulnerabilities to waste, fraud, and abuse*. Washington, DC: Author.

Chaloupka, F. J., Powell, L. M., & Warner, K. E. (2019). The use of excise taxes to reduce tobacco, alcohol, and sugary beverage consumption. *Annual Review of Public Health, 40*, 187–201.

Chingos, M. M., & Blagg, K. (2017). *Making sense of state school funding policy*. Washington, DC: Urban Institute.

Christensen, D. L., Braun, K. V. N., Baio, J., Bilder, D., Charles, J., Constantino, J. N., . . . & Lee, L. C. (2019). Prevalence and characteristics of autism spectrum disorder among children aged 8 years—Autism and developmental disabilities monitoring network. *MMWR Surveillance Summaries, 68*(2), 1–19.

Claxton, G., Rae, M., Long, M., Damico, A., & Whitmore, H. (2019). *Employer health benefits: 2019 annual survey*. Menlo Park, CA: Kaiser Family Foundation.

*Colorado Department of Education. (*2019). *Marijuana tax revenue and education FAQ*. Retrieved from https://www.cde.state.co.us/communications/20170919mjqanda.

Community Development Financial Institutions Coalition. (2019). *Community development financial institutions*. Washington, DC: Author.

Congressional Research Service. (2015). *School construction and renovation: A review of federal programs*. (CRS Report No. R41142). Washington, DC: Author.

Congressional Research Service. (2019). *Federal grants to state and local governments: A historical perspective on contemporary issues* (CRS Report No. R40638). Washington, DC: Author.

Consolidated Appropriations Act, 44 U.S.C. §3516 (2001).

Consolidated Omnibus Budget Reconciliation Act, 29 U.S.C. §§1161–1168 (1985).

Cornman, S. Q., Zhou, L., Howell, M. R., & Young, J. (2018). *Revenues and expenditures for public elementary and secondary education: School year 2015–16 (fiscal year 2016)*. (NCES 2019–301). Washington, DC: National Center for Education Statistics.

Cramer, J., Lemon, M., Wanner, P., & Hicks, C. (2017). *Funding for safety and security in schools: A fifty-state review* (Document number 17–12–2201). Olympia: Washington State Institute for Public Policy.

Dadayan, L., & Auxier, R. (2019, May). *States' growing interest in "sins" despite shrinking sin tax revenues*. PowerPoint presentation at the National Tax Association Annual Spring Symposium, Washington, DC.

Davis, C., Hill, M. E., & Phillips, R. (2019). *Taxing cannabis*. Washington, DC: Institute on Taxation & Economic Policy.

Delgadillo, N. (2018, June). *With shootings on the rise, schools turn to "active shooter" insurance*. Retrieved from http://www.governing.com/topics/education/gov-cost-of-active-shooters-insurance.html.

De Paoli, A., Neary, A., Taft, A., Hughes, B., Gearhart, B., Tolbert, B., . . . Glaros, W. (2017). *Breaking through the status quo: How innovative companies are changing the benefits game to help their employees and boost their bottom line*. Brentwood, TN: Association for Insurance Leadership.

Dunn, H. (2018). *The school business manager's handbook*. Woodbridge, UK: John Cat Educational Ltd.

Economic and Demographic Research. (2019). *2019 Florida tax handbook*. Tallahassee, FL: Author.

EdChoice. (2019). *The ABCs of school choice: 2019 edition*. Indianapolis, IN: Author.

Education Commission of the States. (2018a). *50-State comparison-charter schools: What kind of facilities funding is available to charter schools?* Retrieved from http://ecs.force.com/mbdata/mbquestNB2C?rep=CS1719.

Education Commission of the States. Denver, CO: Author. (2018b). *Nevada school finance study*. Denver, CO: Authors.

Education Infrastructure Act, 20 U.S.C. §§6301 et seq. (1994).

Elementary and Secondary Education Act, 20 U.S.C. §§6301 et seq. (1965).

Emergency Relief Appropriation Act, 15 U.S.C. §728 (1935).

Epple, D., Romano R., & Zimmer, R. (2017). Charter schools: A survey of research on their characteristics and effectiveness. In A. Hanushek, S. J. Machin, & L. Woessmann (Eds.), *Handbook of the economics of education* (Vol. 5, pp. 139–208). Oxford, England: Elsevier.

Family and Medical Leave Act, 29 U.S.C. §§2601 et seq. (1993).

Federation of Tax Administrators. (2017). *Survey of services taxation: Update*. Washington, DC: Author.

Filardo, M. W. (2016). *State of our schools: America's k–12 facilities 2016*. Washington, DC: National Council on School Facilities, 21st Century School Fund, and Center for Green Schools.

Filla, J., Laurene, K., Bland, K., Bland, M., Mikulski, H., Pascarella, T., Stefanak, M., & Hoornbeek, J. (2016). *Resource guide: Health insurance choices for Ohio public entities*. Kent, OH: Center for Public Policy and Health.

Florida Department of Education. (2018). *2018–19 funding for Florida school districts*. Tallahassee, FL: Author.

García, E., & Weiss, E. (2019). *U.S. schools struggle to hire and retain teachers*. Washington, DC: Economic Policy Institute.

Gigliotti, P., & Sorensen, L. C. (2018). Educational resources and student achievement: Evidence from the save harmless provision in New York State. *Economics of Education Review*, *66*, 167–182.

Goel, R. K., Saunoris. J. W., & Schneider, F. (2018). Drivers of the underground economy for over a century: A long term look for the United States. *The Quarterly Review of Economics and Finance*, *71*, 95–106.

Goldstein, A. (2018, January 4). *Trump administration proposes rules for health plans without certain ACA protections*. Retrieved from https://www.washingtonpost.com/national/health-science/trump-administration-proposes-rules-for-health-plans-without-certain-aca-protections.

Gould, J. C. (2015). Tax reform, Congress, and politics. *Tax Notes*, *146*(8), 983–999.

Hamilton, W. A. (n.d.). *To lease or not to lease*. Retrieved from https://www.aasa.org/SchoolAdministratorArticle.aspx?id=15840.

Health Insurance Portability and Accountability Act, 42 U.S.C. §§1320d et seq. (1996).

Hodgin, S. (2019, March 7). *What are the primary drivers of healthcare costs?* Retrieved from http://www.insight-txcin.org/post/what-are-the-primary-drivers-of-healthcare-costs.

House Committee on Appropriations. (2019, April 29). *Appropriations committee releases fiscal year 2020 Labor-HHS-Education Funding Bill*. Retrieved from https://appropriations.house.gov/news/press-releases/appropriations-committee-releases-fiscal-year-2020-labor-hhs-education-funding.

Hunter, M. (2018, March 26). *School funding litigation from coast to coast*. Retrieved from http://www.edlawcenter.org/news/archives/school-funding-national/school-funding-litigation-from-coast-to-coast.html.

Individuals with Disabilities Education Act, 20 U.S.C. §§1400 et seq. (1990, 2004, 2015).

Johnson, S. G. (2019). What constitutes physical loss or damage in a property insurance policy? *Tort Trial & Insurance Practice Law Journal*, *54*(1), 95–124.

Kansel, H. (2019, June 14). *Telemedicine: The cost-effective future of healthcare*. Retrieved from https://www.highpointsolutions.com/telemedicine-cost-effective-future-healthcare/.

Kentucky Department of Education. (2019). *Nickel facts*. Frankfort, KY: Author.

Kerr, M. M., & King, G. (2018). *School crisis prevention and intervention* (2nd ed.). Long Grove, IL: Waveland Press.

King, S., & Bracy, N. L. (2019). School security in the post-Columbine era: Trends, consequences, and future directions. *Journal of Contemporary Criminal Justice*, *35*(3) 274–295.

Kreisman, D., & Steinberg, M. P. (2019). *The effect of increased funding on student achievement: Evidence from Texas's small district adjustment* (Unpublished manuscript). Georgia State University, Atlanta.

Leachman, M., Masterson, K., & Figueroa, E. (2017). *A punishing decade for school funding*. Washington, DC: Center on Budget and Policy Priorities.

Leader, R. (2019, January 3). *How much of your revenue should go to payroll?* Retrieved from https://juiceforbusiness.com/how-much-of-your-revenue-should-go-to-payroll/.

Loughead, K., & Wei, E. (2019). *State individual income tax rates and brackets for 2019*. Washington, DC: Tax Foundation.

Lucki, R. (2017, January 11). *Reimbursable employer solution: The path to avoid state unemployment tax for non-profits*. Retrieved from https://www.corpsyn.com/state-unemployment-tax-non-profits/.

Lueken, M. F., & Shuls, J. V. (2019). *The future of k-12 funding: How states can equalize and make k-12 funding more equitable*. Indianapolis, IN: EdChoice.
Lynch, K. (2019, March). *Why open matters*. PowerPoint presentation at the Connecticut State Colleges and Universities conference, Hartford, Connecticut.
Maestas, G. E. (2017). *Report of unfunded/underfunded mandates: 2017 update*. Plymouth, MA: Plymouth Public Schools.
Martinez, J. C., King, M. P., & Cauchi, R. (2016). *Improving the health care system: Seven state strategies*. Washington, DC: National Conference of State Legislatures.
Martocchio, J. J. (2018). *Employee benefits: A primer for human resource professionals* (6th ed.). New York: McGraw-Hill Education.
McCleery, L. (2019). Purchasing procedures—reminder [memorandum]. Phoenix, AZ: Phoenix Union High School District.
McCord, R. S., & Finnan, L. A. (2019). *2018–19 AASA superintendent salary and benefits study*. Alexandria, VA: ASSA, The School Superintendents Association.
McFarland, J., Hussar, B., Zhang, J., Wang, X., Wang, K., Hein, S., . . . Barmer, A. (2019). *The condition of education 2019* (NCES 2019–144). Washington, DC: National Center for Education Statistics.
McLaren, C. F., Baldwin, M. L., & Boden, L. I. (2018). *Workers' compensation: Benefits, coverage, and costs (2016 data)*. Washington, DC: National Academy of Social Insurance.
Metzer, C., Savoy, C., & Yayboke, E. (2019). *Rethinking taxes and development: Incorporating political economy considerations in DRM strategies*. New York, NY: Rowman and Littlefield.
Michigan Association of School Boards. (2018). *The bargaining toolkit: A resource manual for school districts*. Lansing, MI: Author. Shoop
Milliman, Inc. (2017). *Milliman atlas of public employer health plans*. Seattle, WA: Author.
Munro, M. A., & Murphy, K. A. (2019). *Estate & trust administration for dummies* (2nd ed.). Hoboken, NJ: John Wiley & Sons, Inc.
National Alliance for Public Charter Schools. (2019). *Automatic exemptions from many state and district laws and regulations*. Retrieved from https://www.publiccharters.org/our-work/charter-law-database/components/13.
National Association of State Budget Officers. (2014). *Capital budgeting in the states*. Washington, DC: Author.
National Association of State Budget Officers. (2018). *2018 state expenditure report*. Washington, DC: Author.
National Association of State Procurement Officials. (2018). *2018 survey of state procurement practices*. Lexington, KY: Author.
National Association of State Procurement Officials. (2019). *State and local government procurement: A practical guide* (3rd ed.). Lexington, KY: Author.
National Conference of State Legislatures. (2018, September 16). *State employee health benefits, insurance and costs*. Retrieved from http://www.ncsl.org/research/health/state-employee-health-benefits-ncsl.aspx#Pooled.
National Conference of State Legislatures. (2019a, August 1). *Remote sales tax collection*. Retrieved from http://www.ncsl.org/research/fiscal-policy/e-fairness-legislation-overview.aspx.

National Conference of State Legislatures. (2019b, July 2). *State medical marijuana laws*. Retrieved from http://www.ncsl.org/research/health/state-medical-marijuana-laws.aspx.

National Council on Teacher Quality. (2019, January). *Collective bargaining laws*. Retrieved from https://www.nctq.org/contract-database/collectiveBargaining#map-7.

National Education Association. (2019). *House appropriations committee, FY 2020*. Washington, DC: Author.

National Policy Board for Educational Administration. (2018). *National educational leadership preparation recognition standards: District-level*. Retrieved from www.npbea.org.

New Jersey Association of School Business Officials. (2018). *Anytown public school purchasing manual*. Robbinsville, NJ: Author.

New Jersey Department of Education. (2016). *Protecting your future: Property and liability insurance*. Trenton, NJ: Author.

North Dakota Legislative Council. (2019). *Century code §15.1–36 school construction*. Retrieved from https://www.legis.nd.gov/cencode/t15-1c36.html.

O'Brien, J. M., Blessey-Bickford, M., & Grand, M. M. (2018). *Louisiana Supreme Court issues landmark school decision*. Baton Rouge, LA: McGlinchey Stafford.

Odden, A., & Picus, L. (2020). *School finance: A policy perspective* (6th ed.). New York: McGraw-Hill.

Ohio Auditor Office. (2018). *Ohio compliance supplement*. Columbus, OH: Author.

Ohio School Boards Association. (2018a). *Competitive bidding*. Columbus, OH: Author.

Ohio School Boards Association. (2018b). *District property disposal*. Columbus, OH: Author.

Ohio School Boards Association. (2018c). *Understanding school levies*. Columbus, OH: Author.

Ohio School Facilities Commission. (2019). *Annual report FY 2018*. Columbus, OH: Author.

Ohio School Plan. (2019). *Coverage products offered by the Ohio school plan*. Retrieved from http://www.ohioschoolplan.org/coverages.html.

Parker, E., Diffey, L., & Atchison, B. (2016). *Full-day kindergarten: A look across the states*. Denver, CO: Education Commission of the States.

Parker, E., Diffey, L., & Atchison, B. (2018). *How states fund pre-k: A primer for policymakers*. Denver, CO: Education Commission of the States.

Patient Protection and Affordable Care Act, 42 U.S.C. §§18001 et seq. (2010).

The Pew Charitable Trusts. (2016). *State retiree health spending*. Philadelphia, PA: Author.

The Pew Charitable Trusts. (2019a). *Legal protections for state pension and retiree health benefits*. Philadelphia, PA: Author.

The Pew Charitable Trusts. (2019b, June 4). *"Lost decade" casts a post-recession shadow on state finances*. Retrieved from https://www.pewtrusts.org/en/research-and-analysis/issue-briefs/2019/06/lost-decade-casts-a-post-recession-shadow-on-state-finances.

Picus, Odden, & Associates. (2019, May 18). *State studies*. Retrieved from http://picusodden.com/state-studies/.

PlanCon Advisory Committee. (2018). *Public school building construction and reconstruction advisory committee final report*. Harrisburg, PA: Author.
Reuters Staff. (2018, April 10). *States shift funding for school safety after Parkland shooting*. Retrieved from https://www.reuters.com/article/us-usa-guns-education-funding-factbox/factbox-states-shift-funding-for-school-safety-after-parkland-shooting-idUSKBN1HH2NG.
Richmond, E. (2019, April 22). *When school districts can't raise funds for facilities*. Retrieved from https://hechingerreport.org/when-school-districts-cant-raise-funds-for-facilities/.
Riley, T., Schneiter, E., Hensley-Quinn, M., Cousart, C., & Horvath, J. (2019). *Cross-agency strategies to curb health care costs: Leveraging state purchasing power*. Portland, ME: National Academy for State Health Policy.
Rubin, I. S. (2017). *The politics of public budgeting: Getting and spending, borrowing and balancing* (8th ed.). Washington, DC: CQ Press.
Scheve, K., & Stasavage, D. (2019). *Equal treatment and the inelasticity of tax policy to rising inequality* (Unpublished manuscript). Stanford University, Stanford.
Schilling, C. A., & Tomal, D. R. (2019). *School finance and business management: Optimizing fiscal, facility and human resources* (2nd ed.). New York: Rowman and Littlefield.
Schmitz, K., & Aldeman, C. (2017). *Retirement reality check: Grading state teacher pension plans*. Washington, DC: Bellwether Education Partners.
SchoolFunding.Info. (2019). *Overview of litigation history*. Retrieved from http://schoolfunding.info/litigation-map.
Shell, G. R. (2019). *Bargaining for advantage: Negotiation strategies for reasonable people*. London, UK: Penguin Press.
Shoop, J. (March, 2019). *Public school purchasing: A cornucopia of compliance*. Paper presented at the New Jersey Association of School Business Officials workshop, Robbinsville, New Jersey.
Sisko, A. M., Keehan, S. P., Poisal, J. A., Cuckler, G. A., Smith, S. D., Madison, A. J., . . . & Hardesty, J. C. (2019). National health expenditure projections, 2018–27: Economic and demographic trends drive spending and enrollment growth. *Health Affairs*, *38*(3), 491–501.
Sjoquist, D. L. (2019). *New normal? The declining relative importance of state taxes* (Working Paper No. 10–03). Atlanta, GA: The Center for State and Local Finance.
Slutsky, B. (2017). *Strategies to guide your textbook adoption in history-social science*. Oakland, CA: Regents of the University of California.
Sneha, E., García, J. L., Heckman, J. J., & Hojman, A. (2017). Early childhood education. In R. A. Moffitt (Ed.), *Economics of means: Tested transfer programs in the United States* (Vol. II, pp. 235–297). Chicago, IL: University of Chicago Press.
Snyder, T. D., de Brey, C. & Dillow, S. A. (2019). *Digest of education statistics, 2017* (NCES 2018–070). Washington, DC: National Center for Education Statistics.
Social Security Act, 42 U.S.C. §§301–1305 (1935).
Social Security Amendments, 42 U.S.C. §1305 (1965).
South Carolina Public Benefits Authority. (2018). *2019 insurance benefits guide*. Columbia, SC: Author.

South Dakota v Wayfair, Inc., 138 S. Ct. 2080 (2018).

Sweetman, C. (2018, December 10). *Norman public schools says not enough money to cover all bus crash victims' bills*. Retrieved from https://kfor.com/2018/12/10/norman-public-schools-says-not-enough-money-to-cover-all-bus-crash-victims-bills.

Szymendera, S. D. (2017). *Workers' compensation: Overview and issues* (CRS Report No. R44580). Washington, DC: Congressional Research Service.

Taxpayers for Public Education v Douglas County School District, 137 U.S. 232 (2017).

Texas Association of Counties. (2019). *The cost of county government: 2018 unfunded mandates survey*. Austin, TX: Author.

Texas Association of School Administrators and Texas Association of School Boards. (2018). *Report on unfunded mandates: Cost drivers in public education*. Austin, TX: Authors.

Texas Association of School Boards. (2018). *The board's role in risk management*. Austin, TX: Author.

Texas Association of School Boards. (2019). *Purchasing cooperatives*. Austin, TX: Author.

Texas Education Agency. (2019a). *Existing debt allocation program*. Austin, TX: Author.

Texas Education Agency. (2019b). *Financial accountability system resource guide—Module 5: Purchasing*. Austin, TX: Author.

Thompson, G. (2017, October 20). *The shifting textbook adoption market*. Retrieved from https://victoryprd.com/blog/shifting-textbook-adoption-market/.

Transportation of Pupils, 14 Del. C. Ch. 29 § 2904 (1953).

Unemployment Tax Act, 26 U.S.C. §3301 (1939).

Uniformed Services Employment and Reemployment Rights Act, 38 U.S.C. §§4301–4335 (1994).

U.S. Census Bureau. (2019a, May 2). *2017 Public elementary-secondary education finance data*. Retrieved from https://www.census.gov/data/tables/2017/econ/school-finances/secondary-education-finance.html.

U.S. Census Bureau. (2019b, June 11). *2018 Annual survey of state government tax collections by category table*. Retrieved from https://www.census.gov/data/tables/2018/econ/stc/2018-annual.html.

U.S. Department of Education. (2019). *Fiscal year 2020 budget summary and background information*. Washington, DC: Author.

U.S. Department of Labor. (2018, July 16). *Consumer prices up 2.9 percent over 12 months ended June 2018*. Retrieved from https://www.bls.gov/opub/ted/2018/consumer-prices-up-2-point-9-percent-over-12-months-ended-june-2018.htm.

U.S. Department of Labor. (2019a). *Comparison of state unemployment insurance laws*. Washington, DC: Author.

U.S. Department of Labor. (2019b). *Employer costs for employee compensation: March 2019*. Washington, DC: Author.

U.S. Department of Labor. (2019c). *National compensation survey: Employee benefits in the United States, March 2019*. Washington, DC: Author.

Vines, D., Braceland, A., Rollins, E., & Miller, S. (2018). *Comprehensive health insurance: Billing, coding, and reimbursement* (3rd ed.). Upper Saddle River, NJ: Pearson Education, Inc.

Weglarz-Ward, J., Ang, C., & Gaynes, R. (2019). Supporting high quality early childhood experiences for children with and without disabilities and their families in Nevada. *Policy Issues in Nevada education*, *3*(1), 11–19.

Weiner, K. G., & Green, P. C. (2018). *Private school vouchers: Legal challenges and civil rights protections* (Working Paper). Los Angeles, CA: UCLA Civil Rights Project.

Wiehe, M., Davis, A, Davis, C., Gardner, M., Christensen Gee, L., & Grundman, D. (2018). *Who pays? A distributional analysis of the tax systems in all 50 states* (6th ed.). Washington, DC: The Institute on Taxation & Economic Policy.

Williams, E. (2017). *A four-point fiscal policy blueprint for building thriving state economies*. Washington, DC: Center on Budget and Policy Priorities.

Wood, R. C., Thompson, D. C., & Crampton, F. E. (2019). *Money and schools* (7th ed.). New York, NY: Routledge.

Worth, M. J. (2019). *Nonprofit management: Principles and practice* (5th ed.). Thousand Oaks, CA: Sage Publications, Inc.

Yudof, M. G. (1991). School finance reform in Texas: The Edgewood saga. *Harvard Journal on Legislation*, *28*(2), 499–505.

Zelman v Simmons-Harris, 536 U.S. 639 (2002).

Ziebarth, T. (2019). *State policy snapshot: Facility funding for public charter schools*. Washington, DC: National Alliance for Public Charter Schools.

Index

About the Author

Dr. Clinton Born is a thirty-year veteran of public schools where he served as a superintendent of schools, principal, assistant principal, guidance counselor, and teacher. Currently, he is a professor at the Franciscan University of Steubenville graduate education program teaching courses to prepare aspiring public and nonpublic school administrators for licensure. Throughout his distinguished career, he

- stewarded a school district from financial ruin to fiscal stability,
- inherited a massive district health insurance debt and reversed that situation to a healthy positive balance by implementing various strategies explained in this text,
- initiated and directed many district facility renovations, and
- witnessed and experienced the fiscal troubles that plague school officials.

Printed in Great Britain
by Amazon